the

BUTLER

the BUTLER

A WITNESS TO HISTORY

WIL HAYGOOD

37INK

—

ATRIA

New York   London   Toronto   Sydney   New Delhi

37INK

ATRIA

An Imprint of Simon & Schuster, Inc.
1230 Avenue of the Americas
New York, NY 10020

First 37 INK/Atria Paperback edition January 2018

37INK / ATRIA PAPERBACK and colophon are trademarks of Simon & Schuster, Inc.

Personal photos of the Allen family courtesy of Charles Allen. Production and set photos from *Lee Daniels' The Butler* courtesy of Pamela Williams Productions. Photograph of President Dwight D. Eisenhower courtesy of Dwight D. Eisenhower Presidential Library and Museum. Photograph of President John F. Kennedy courtesy of National Archives and Records Administration. Photograph of President Lyndon B. Johnson courtesy of Lyndon Baines Johnson Library and Museum. Photograph of President Richard M. Nixon courtesy of Richard Nixon Presidential Library and Museum. Photograph of President Ronald Reagan courtesy of Ronald Reagan Presidential Library. Photograph of President Barack Obama courtesy of the White House.

For information about special discounts for bulk purchases, please contact Simon & Schuster Special Sales at 1-866-506-1949 or business@simonandschuster.com.

The Simon & Schuster Speakers Bureau can bring authors to your live event. For more information or to book an event, contact the Simon & Schuster Speakers Bureau at 1-866-248-3049 or visit our website at www.simonspeakers.com.

Designed by Kyoko Watanabe

Manufactured in the United States of America

10   9   8   7   6   5   4   3   2

Library of Congress Cataloging-in-Publication Data is available.

ISBN 978-1-4767-5299-0
ISBN 978-1-5011-9560-0 (pbk)
ISBN 978-1-4767-5327-0 (ebook)

This book is dedicated to the memory of
Laura Ziskin

CONTENTS

FOREWORD

WHILE THE MOVIE *The Butler* is set against historical events, the title character and his family are fictionalized. From the moment I read Wil Haygood's article about him in the *Washington Post*, I was very moved by the real life of Eugene Allen. I remember Wil Haygood sharing with me his inspiration for writing his original article. On the cusp of Obama's election he sought to find an African American butler who had seen firsthand the civil rights movement from both within and outside the White House. Wil knocked on Mr. Allen's door and was greeted by a humble and elegant man and his gracious wife, who spent the afternoon sharing stories and showing treasure troves of memorabilia discreetly lining the walls of his basement.

When I first read Danny Strong's screenplay of *The Butler,* I knew I had to direct this film. Inspired by films like *Gone with the Wind,* I thought if I could capture even half of what that film accomplished, I would be onto something magical. But, most important, I saw a way to frame the story: I'd contrast the history of the times, particularly the fight for civil rights equality, against what would become the heart of the film, the evolution of a father-son relationship. While the father witnessed directly the role each president played in dictating the course of civil rights, the son rebelled against what he perceived as the subservience of his father. He aggressively took his fight for equality to the streets, even if it meant sacrificing his life. In the end, this is a story of healing, both for our nation and most importantly for father and son, as each man came to respect the pivotal and essential role the other played in the course of changing history. This is the emotional and universal anchor of this movie and subject matter I very much wanted to explore.

And while this father and son and family are fictional characters, we were able to borrow some extraordinary moments from Eugene's real life to weave into the movie—such as the grieving Jacqueline Kennedy giving one of the slain president's ties to the butler, and Nancy Reagan inviting the butler and his wife to a state dinner. Eugene Allen was a remarkable man, and I am happy and grateful that Wil Haygood had the passion and perseverance to find him and to bring his story to life in his article and through this book, which expands the story.

the BUTLER

THE BUTLER'S JOURNEY

H E WAS OUT there somewhere. By now he'd be an old man. He had worked "decades" in the White House. Maybe he had passed away virtually alone, and there had been only a wisp of an obituary notice. But no one could confirm if that were so. Maybe I was looking for a ghost. Actually, I was looking for a butler. I couldn't stop looking.

Yes, a butler.

It is such an old-fashioned and anachronistic term: *the butler.* Someone who serves people, who sees but doesn't see; someone who can read the moods of the people he serves. The figure in the shadows. Movie lovers fell in love with the butler as a cinematic figure in the 1936 film *My Man Godfrey,* which starred William Powell as the butler of a chaotic household. More recently, the butler figure and other backstage players have been popularized in the beloved television series *Downton Abbey*. My butler was a gentleman by the name of Eugene Allen. For thirty-four years, he had been a butler at the house located in Washington, DC, at 1600 Pennsylvania Avenue, which the world knows as the White House.

Finally, after talking to many, many people, on both coasts of the country, and making dozens and dozens of phone calls, I found him. He was very much alive. He was living with his wife, Helene, on a quiet street in Northwest Washington. Eugene Allen had worked—as a butler—in eight presidential administrations, from Harry Truman's to Ronald Reagan's. He was both a witness to history and unknown to it.

"Come right in," he said, opening the door to his home on that cold November day in 2008. He had already taken his morning medications. He had already served his wife breakfast. He was eighty-nine years old, and he was about to crack history open for me in a whole new way.

This is how the story of a White House butler—who would land in newsprint the world over after a story I had written appeared on the front page of the *Washington Post* three days after the historic election on November 4, 2008, of Barack Obama—actually unspooled.

———

IT ALL BEGAN in summery darkness in 2008, down in Chapel Hill, North Carolina. Midnight had come and gone, and the speech was being summed up and analyzed and written about. Yet another Democratic presidential hopeful had been pleading with a throng of students and voters about why they should vote for him. The rafters of what is known as the Dean Dome on the campus of the University of North Carolina were packed. The candidate, who possessed a smooth and confident disposition, was on his way. The audience was multiracial, young and old. The instantly recognizable guttural voice of Stevie Wonder was jumping from the loudspeakers. Some of the old in attendance were veterans of the movement, as in civil rights movement: the sixties, segregation, those brave souls gunned down and buried all across the South. Now the candidate was before them, shirtsleeves rolled up, holding the microphone. "I'm running because of what Dr. King called the fierce urgency of now, because I believe in such a thing as being too late, and that hour, North Carolina, is upon us." The words had a churchy, movement feel to them, and then–senator Barack Obama was effortlessly lifting the throng up out of their seats. The noise and clapping pointed to believers. But still, it was the South, he was a black man, the White House seemed a bit of a fantastical dream. History and demons were everywhere, though the candidate seemed impervious to all that.

I was one of the writers covering the Obama campaign that night for the *Washington Post,* flying in and out of a slew of states over a seven-day period. Following the Chapel Hill rally and speech—and after I'd interviewed a few folks inside—it was time to move outside and head for the bus, which would take us journalists back to the hotel. The night air was sweet and rather lovely. Suddenly, I heard the oddest thing: cries, and coming from nearby. I turned my head and squinted through the dark. Just over there, on a bench, sat three young ladies—college students. I stepped toward them and asked if anything was wrong, if there was anything I could do. "Our fathers won't speak to us," one of them said through her sobs, "because we support that man in there." They had all been inside the Dome. The speaker's cohorts nodded through reddened eyes. She went on: "Our fathers don't want us supporting a black man, but they can't stop us." Their words stilled me. I sat talking with them for a while. Their sobs faded away, and the looks on their faces soon returned to a kind of resplendent defiance. They were staring down their daddies; they were going to be a part of the movement to get this black man to the White House. Maybe I was half-exhausted, maybe I was in a dreamy state of mind, maybe those tears had touched me deeper than I knew. But then and there, in that southern darkness—as if I had been kicked by a mule—I told myself that Barack Obama was indeed going to get to 1600 Pennsylvania Avenue, to the White House.

Just days after that night in Chapel Hill, I told Steve Reiss, my editor, that Barack Obama was going to win the presidency, and because he was going to win, I needed to find someone from the era of segregation, and find them right now, to write about what this upcoming and momentous event in American history would mean to them. And I wanted the person to have worked in the White House, I told him. My editor's eyebrows arched. "Hmm." Reiss sighed. He didn't believe Obama would win, but he did believe my intentions. He wanted me to finish a couple of other hanging assignments, then I could go in search of this ghostly person. He wondered: how far back would I look for this White House employee? "Are you talking the nineteen sixties?"

"Farther back," I said.

I wanted to find a black man or woman who had worked and scrubbed inside the White House, who had washed dishes there, who had drunk from those COLORED ONLY water fountains in America during the Jim Crow years. I did not mind that people around me were constantly saying America would not elect a black man as president.

A black employee at the White House in the 1950s? The White House operator told me it was their policy not to give out names of former employees, and she knew of no White House office that would assist me in such an endeavor. There are always walls, roadblocks in a reporter's work, and I told myself this was nothing to fret about. Besides, I had a source on Capitol Hill, in a congressman's office, someone who would help. But after much back-and-forth, this source couldn't gain any guidance from the White House either. Others were soon offering blank stares, or long pauses on the telephone, with no possible names or even leads. Then, with me wondering if such a person could be found, someone told me about a lady in Florida who used to work at the White House, who might know of just such a person.

The woman in Florida, a former White House employee, gave me a name. "If he'd have passed away I would have heard about it," she said. "The last time I saw Eugene Allen he was standing outside of 1600 Pennsylvania Avenue, getting into a taxicab. He was attending a reunion at the White House. He worked there many years as a butler." She did not know exactly how many years.

If Eugene Allen were still alive, I had to find him. If he had been getting into a taxi when last seen by my Florida contact, that meant he likely lived in the Washington, DC–Maryland–Virginia region. The phone books were full of Eugene Allens. By the time I had made forty calls without tracking down this particular Eugene Allen, I began to wonder if this man still lived in the area. People age and become snow-birds. They move to California, Arizona, Florida. And, of course, they die. The unsuccessful calls kept mounting.

"Hello, I'm looking for Mr. Eugene Allen, who used to work as a butler at the White House." It was about the fifty-sixth call.

"You're speaking to him."

The subway train rumbled under the surface of DC. The butler had given directions to his home. It was a working-class neighborhood through and around which the 1960s riots had once swept. On my way to his street I walked past a fish fry joint, and storefront churches, and small clothing stores. In front of the butler's home, the front gate had been left noticeably ajar: expecting company.

"Come right in," Eugene Allen said. His back was slightly bent, and he stepped about with little grimaces. He introduced Helene, his wife, who was reclining in an easy chair with her cane lying across her lap. She was smiling warmly. They lived alone. After he was seated, both were quick to let me know that they'd talk with me, but only after they watched their beloved game show, *The Price Is Right.* They watched back-to-back episodes, watched them with an intensity that told me not to dare interrupt, so I didn't.

Splayed on an end table were half a dozen magazines with then–Senator Barack Obama's picture. It was easy to tell how proud they were of his candidacy. As game show images flickered on the wide-screen television (a gift from their only child, Charles, a Vietnam War vet who worked as an investigator with the State Department), I saw on a wall the only picture that hinted at employment at the White House: the Allens standing with President and Nancy Reagan at what seemed a very formal affair. I still was unsure of exactly how many presidents Eugene Allen had worked for.

"Eight presidents," he told me.

Eight? He could tell I was surprised.

"That's right. Eight. Started with Harry Truman and worked all the way up to President Reagan."

He started telling me about his life. Born in 1919 in Scottsville, Virginia, on a plantation, he grew up working as a "house boy" for a white family. They taught him kitchen skills, and he came of age washing dishes and setting tables for that family. There was nary a hint of bitterness in his voice about his upbringing. But like Huck Finn, he wanted to light out for the territory. He got as far as Hot Springs, Virginia, home to the renowned Homestead Resort. With his refined skills, he got a job there as a waiter.

In the 1930s, jobs for Negroes anywhere quickly spread on a grapevine that was stitched together by church members, Pullman porters, bellhops at Negro hotels—the vanguard of what would form the backbone of the black working and middle class. While in Hot Springs, someone told Eugene Allen about a job in Washington, DC, at a country club. He'd heard about the high steppers and good tips at country clubs. He threw his suits in a trunk and soon found himself in the nation's capital.

The Depression lay like a hard stone across the land, but he had a job in Washington, and he liked it. He wore nice suits, hats with soft brims, and two-toned shoes. (In some photos that survive from the era, there he is, sitting on the hood of a car, in a natty suit and fedora, looking like a million bucks though flat broke.) At a party one night in 1942 he met Helene, also a transplant to DC. She had relatives in Washington who sent letters and magazines to the small town in North Carolina where she was born and raised. Desperate to get out of the Jim Crow South, she begged her father to let her go live in this mecca her relatives described. Though he initially said no, she kept asking until he finally relented. Now in DC, she and Eugene were eyeballing one another across the music and bobbing heads at a nighttime soirée; she thought surely he'd ask for her phone number. It was a wartime city, and moments were precious. Life was so unpredictable. But he was too shy. "So I tracked his number down," she says. They both chuckle. They married a year after meeting.

By 1947 they had saved enough to purchase their home on Otis Place in the city. Eugene was working at the country club. The job required a certain degree of smoothness, of discretion, and those were traits he possessed, traits that gained him favorable attention from the politicians and bankers who belonged to the country club. Five years later, in 1952, someone at the country club told him they were looking for "pantry workers" over at the White House, and that he should go over there and talk with Alonzo Fields. "I wasn't even looking for a job," he told me.

Fields, a black man, had risen from butler to maître d' at the White House. An Indiana native, he had trained at the New England Conservatory of Music in hopes of teaching someday. When his benefactor died, his music dreams were thwarted, so he had made ends meet by working as a waiter. He joined the White House staff during the Hoover administration and would work there for twenty-one years under four presidents. He had no earthly idea that Eugene Allen, the man sitting before him, would far surpass him in number of presidents worked for and years served.

Fields talked to Allen about the prestige of working at the White

House, how discretion was to be valued and practiced. Fields must have picked up on Allen's air of quiet dignity because he hired him to work in the pantry. The starting salary was twenty-four hundred dollars a year. In 1952, it was decent money. Helene, a vivacious sort, now owned bragging rights: her husband worked at 1600 Pennsylvania Avenue, a fact she was quick to drop on neighbors and fellow churchgoers. It bestowed a certain importance on the Allen family.

Allen admits he was quite nervous when Fields came looking for him one day shortly after he began work at the White House. He told Allen it was time to meet President Harry Truman. "Just listen to this man," Truman said to Allen, pointing his finger in the direction of Alonzo Fields, "and you'll be okay." The years began to roll by. Allen was promoted to full-fledged butler. To celebrate that and other occasions, he and Helene would throw little dinner parties down in their basement, which was fairly stark save for a noticeable black-and-white portrait of Jackie Robinson, which hung on a wall near the bar. They'd be joined by fellow butlers and their wives, neighbors, and acquaintances from their church. Mixed drinks would be served and folks would start, after a week of being buttoned-up, to relax. Guests would plead around the card table and makeshift bar for any information about what went on at the White House. Eugene was ever tight-lipped.

After having left the White House all these years later, Eugene Allen was more open. He admitted he could hardly have envisioned how history would evolve during his years—thirty-four in all—spent at the White House. He reminisced about shaking the hand of every president he had worked for, and about spending nights in the White House when the weather forbade his getting home. He reminisced about flying on *Air Force One,* and about all the Easter egg hunts for the children. He talked about all the state dinners and White House luncheons.

"I was there, honey," Helene pipes in. They both smile: old souls, old love.

During the tense Little Rock school desegregation crisis, he watched President Eisenhower argue with Arkansas governor Orval Faubus over the phone. It made him mighty proud when Eisenhower sent in federal troops to protect the black schoolchildren. He was there when President Kennedy had to protect James Meredith on the campus of the University of Mississippi in 1963 as the school, by court order, was forced to allow the first black student to enroll. The stories come more frequently now, but back then, when Helene would ask him about the social and racial strife engulfing the country and what it was doing to the president he was serving, Eugene Allen was mostly silent.

There were sweeter moments. He was there, at the White House, in 1963 when President Kennedy hosted an event to honor the one-hundredth anniversary of the Emancipation Proclamation. Allen and the other butlers had never seen so many blacks at the White House at one time, upwards of eight hundred floating about, among them

Langston Hughes and Sammy Davis Jr. (One of the black guests cracked it was like being inside Uncle Tom's cabin.) Sometimes, on getting back to the White House kitchen, where he'd pause for a break, he'd shake his head at the wonder of social progress: Allen himself had been born in the former Confederacy and only fifty-four years after the end of slavery.

We know, of course, the Kennedy years would come to a tragic end. When President Kennedy was shot in Dallas, Allen and the other crestfallen butlers awaited the arrival back at the White House of those who had traveled with Kennedy. He remembers First Lady Jackie Kennedy being in a near-catatonic state, and there were the low-pitched voices of the Kennedy children that seemed particularly sad. When Allen went home on the night of the Kennedy assassination, he felt strongly that he should get back to the White House; he could not sleep. He prepared to return. Helene cautioned him about going out so late, with so little rest. But he was determined. As he was putting on his coat in the hallway, he collapsed into sobs. Charles, the son, would later tell me that was the first and only time he had seen his father cry. Indeed, Kennedy enjoyed an almost gospel-like devotion from blacks in America.

It pained Eugene Allen to see a White House engulfed in such deep and dark sadness. He saw it everywhere: in the butlers' quarters, in the White House kitchen, in the West Wing. Kennedy was the president who had begun to take on the intransigent Southern Democrats in his own political party over the issue of civil rights. And he was the president who had hosted gatherings at the White House that included more blacks than ever before. Now a gunman had taken him away.

One of Eugene Allen's unique gifts as a White House butler—who seemed to gain more respect with each incoming administration—was his ability to improvise. In the days following the assassination, he wanted to bring a bit of cheer to the White House; he was especially worried about the Kennedy children, John and Caroline. It had been a long time since there had been such youth in the White House, and the nation had fawned over the children as they romped into the arms of their father. Eugene Allen told the White House chef to whip up some goodies: he was going to have a party for John and Caroline and some of their little friends. And there they were, all seated around a little table, enjoying themselves, smiling, the butler bending and serving. For a little while at least, there was the cacophony of little voices squealing with delight. Even the butler found reason to smile.

The butler thought President Johnson brave, if somewhat vulgar with his language. Yes, there were times, plenty of times, when Eugene Allen wanted to march right up to President Johnson and tell him about his boy, Charles, who had been sent to Vietnam, who was sweating in jungle darkness, who was trying to stay alive and get his ass back home. But Eugene Allen was caught in the middle, like a figurine bobbing on turbulent waves: he had to balance his concerns about being tossed out of the White House for insubordination on the one hand and his and Helene's worries about their only son being half a world away, trying to stay alive, on the other. The father, the butler, watching history turn, could not say a word. All he could do was stand there, frozen, as Johnson talked to his so-called brilliant war hawks—Robert McNamara and McGeorge Bundy and Dean Rusk—and howled about sending more, more, more troops. Of President Richard Nixon, he'd only say he was shrewd, a little secretive, and a bit distant—the telltale traits, as it were, that would come to doom the Nixon presidency.

On weekends in Washington, the butler sometimes played golf on the Langston Golf Course. That led to chats with President Ford, a golfer himself. Eugene Allen and Ford also shared the same birthdays. "It's Gene's birthday, too!" First Lady Betty Ford would call out when they'd bring the cake out to surprise her husband. Soon as Eugene put his key in the door, and she had presented him with his birthday gifts, Helene just had to know what Mrs. Ford had given the president for his birthday.

In 1980, while serving in the Reagan administration, Eugene Allen was promoted to maître d', a position of power among the butlers and maids at the White House. (He had outlasted so many other butlers, doubling the number of presidents for whom Alonzo Fields—the man who hired him—had worked.) Allen couldn't help but feel the tension in the Reagan White House over the issue of apartheid in South Africa. Many American blacks from the civil rights movement joined with liberal whites—there were a good number of Republican politicians as well—in assailing the Reagan administration for supporting the apartheid regime. But White House butlers did not dare enter the political fray. They worked to improve the lot of their families by showing up to work every day. In all his years—thirty-four years and eight presidents—Eugene Allen never missed a day of work. Even during the 1960s riots, when it was hard to drive through the streets of Washington, he made it to work, and on foot if he had to.

One afternoon, inside the Reagan White House, Eugene Allen saw Nancy Reagan coming in his direction. There was an upcoming state dinner for West German chancellor Helmut Kohl. He imagined she wanted him to attend to some last-minute details. Instead, Nancy Reagan told Eugene Allen he would not be needed at the state dinner. He was suddenly dumbfounded. Before he could say anything, she told him that he and his wife, Helene, would be attending the state dinner—as guests of the president, in honor of his decades-long service to the White House and the presidents he had served. He was deeply touched, could barely move. He could imagine the look on his wife's face when she heard they were going to a state dinner together. He was one of the first butlers in the history of the White House to be invited to a state dinner as a guest—a guest just like the ambassadors and business magnates who received invitations to such affairs.

Helene recalled how nervous she was about the pending state dinner, about what clothes and jewelry to wear. She had expressed worry to friends and fretted to her son, Charles, about what in the world she would talk about. She'd never gone to college, after all. Despite her insecurities, on the night of the dinner, she and Eugene looked resplendent leaving the house. Helene's jewelry gleamed. Neighbors stared at them wide-eyed.

That night, Eugene Allen walked in the front door of the White House—not through the back entrance where service workers entered. Amid the glamour and splendor, they were in awe. "Had champagne that night," the butler's wife would remember all these years later. As she said it, Eugene, rocking in his chair, just grinned: for so many years he had stocked the champagne at the White House.

As if out of respect for that very special night, Eugene and Helene Allen had only one picture on the wall in their home that spoke of his White House years. It was the picture of them walking through the receiving line at the White House during the state dinner. The plantation of his boyhood years must have seemed a lifetime ago.

Frankly, from the moment I entered the Allens' home, I was surprised there were not more visual highlights of his White House career. In Washington, people hang and frame all manner of photographs and documents.

After hours had passed during my first visit, and we'd exhausted ourselves with talk and their memories, Helene said to her husband, "You can show him now," while nodding in my direction.

Eugene Allen slowly stood up. He asked me to follow him from the living room to the kitchen, stopping in front of a door—the basement door. His long and bony right arm reached onto his belt loop, where a string of keys jangled. He unlocked the door. I wondered why anyone had to keep their basement door locked. Then I quickly mused it was a gritty neighborhood; they were elderly and lived alone. "Follow me," he said. "And hold on to my arm. The light switch is in the middle of the basement."

We descended creaky stairs and walked into pitch blackness at the bottom of the stairwell. He inched his way to the hanging overhead string and pulled it. "Well, here it is," he said, as I began scanning the now bright room, stunned as my gaze moved from wall to wall at what I was seeing: there were rich, gorgeous pictures on the wall of Eugene Allen with President Kennedy, with President Eisenhower, with President Nixon. He pointed to a picture of him with Sammy Davis Jr. Another with him and Duke Ellington and some other butlers. He pulled me to another corner of the basement. "Ike painted this picture for me," he said. There were framed letters from the presidents to him on his birthday. It was like being dropped into a museum. There were hundreds and hundreds of pieces of memorabilia.

We heard shuffling feet walking across the kitchen floor. It was Helene.

"Show him the picture of us with Ella Fitzgerald!" she hollered down at us.

"Give me time. I am. Give me time," the butler called up to her. His eyes were lit; he was smiling as if he suddenly appreciated the gallantry and perseverance of his own life. He shifted things so I could get better views. There were marbled busts of the presidents he had worked for; there were pictures of state dinners with Eugene Allen hovering in the background. On a shelf there were several four-inch photo albums. Inside them were some of the most gorgeous pictures of White House dining I had ever seen. The lit candles in the photos nearly flickered off the pages. There were framed and signed letters from the presidents to him and his wife. There were also several boxes of old *Look* and *Life* magazines. Helene, who helped curate the collection, had made especially sure to keep anything with Jackie Kennedy on the cover. It was a visual feast. Of course this basement needed to be locked. These were treasures, likely bound for a museum somewhere, someday. A life lived in the hard shadow of power. A life lived inside the White House during the Korean War, the Cold War, Little Rock, Rosa Parks on the move, the Cuban missile crisis, the moon landing, the integration of Ole Miss, Vietnam, the murders of Medgar Evers, Martin Luther King Jr., Malcolm X, and the taken-from-us Kennedy brothers. Also, Watergate. (How the teacups must have rattled inside the White House then.) And the rise of George Wallace and Barry Goldwater, two men linked to political movements that terrified blacks.

He stepped closer to another picture hanging on the wall and squinted: it was a sepia-toned and nearly faded photograph of him and

Ike at Gettysburg—after Ike had left the White House. These had been lasting relationships. It is hard to imagine that some of these presidents didn't admire the life of Eugene Allen, how he had survived, stayed off the unemployment rolls, navigated the politics of each administration. The children of several presidents still had him on their Christmas card list. He kept turning in the basement, as if on an easel, a world of power and glitter that had spun all around him, with him taking a place inside it.

In time, he pulled the light switch, returning the basement to darkness. Helene was awaiting us at the top of the stairs, leaning on her cane. I told her that what I had seen in the basement—his life, their life—had simply stunned me. "Hmm-mmm," she said, nodding in agreement.

Back in the living room there were more photographs to look at. More memories that tumbled out: that time the White House had sent a Lincoln Town Car right to their home in the predawn darkness to ferry the butler to Andrews Air Force Base to hop aboard *Air Force One*; tales about the dexterity it took to serve a first-class meal on a plane zooming through the skies with the leader of the free world on board: Balance the tray with the wineglasses just so! Don't let the gravy roll from the plate! And Lord have mercy, don't trip and fall in the aisle of the plane. They both chuckled inside their warm house.

Helene, who had her own special memories, had kept hold of all those pretty dresses and lovely hats she had worn to White House events. They just could never imagine giving the clothing away. Sometimes Helene would implore Eugene to creep down into the basement and retrieve one of those magazines with Jackie on the cover. And she'd get to flipping through it in the lamplight and they'd both share some memories about being eyewitnesses to Camelot.

My visit was coming to an end. The election was looming just days away. It was so easy to feel how eager the Allens, who lived an unassuming life on this ordinary street in Washington, DC, were to vote. Elderly people, from the South, they had once been denied the right to vote. And now all their hopes and memories—of being colored, then Negro, then black, then that epithet hurled from certain corners, now African American—were rolling toward one candidate, Barack Obama. It was as if they were rocking Barack Obama into their very bosoms.

I left and felt, walking away from this modest dwelling, that I certainly had quite a unique story to tell. Actually, I wanted to run back once I reached the corner and plead with them to keep that basement locked, to keep those treasures safe.

Over the weekend, a nation kept wondering, kept asking: Would America elect a black man its president? My own family members back in Ohio weighed in: no, Obama would not win this time; America was not yet ready, maybe two election cycles away.

On Sunday night—thirty-six hours before Election Day—Charles Allen came over to visit his parents. He thought they'd bombard him with questions about the new, flat-screen television he had recently bought them. What did this button do? And what about that one? Instead, Helene couldn't wait to tell her son that a writer had come to visit two days earlier. "She was so happy," Charles would tell me. "She felt somebody was finally going to tell Eugene's story. She said to me, before going to bed, 'I feel so at peace.' " Charles would later tell a reporter in Ohio that it seemed "preordained" for me to come by.

The next morning, Monday, I phoned them. Just to say hello and inquire about the photographer sent to take their picture for my story. "She's gone," Eugene said, referring to Helene. His voice sounded strange, hollow even. I asked where she had gone. "I woke up and my wife didn't," he explained. I was still confused. Gone to the hospital? No, he said, Helene had passed in the night. I was speechless and suddenly felt woozy. I asked if there was anyone with him. Some church ladies were just then coming through the door.

Amid the sadness, as the hours passed, some visitors—among them current and former White House butlers and maids and dishwashers—began to share stories about the beautiful Helene Allen: how she loved to dance; how she just loved champagne; the way she looked in her dresses when heading off for some grand function at the White House. Meanwhile, amid this sudden pain, they'd have to constantly shove Eugene out of the kitchen; he kept wanting to serve everyone. After half a century of butlerlike duties, he could not step back and leave the work to others.

Twenty-four hours later Eugene Allen, retired White House butler, rose in the darkness, got dressed in a semi-blur of confusion—his wife of sixty-five years gone, her *Jet, Ebony,* and *Newsweek* magazines with covers picturing presidential candidate Barack Obama still on the living room coffee table—to go vote. It must have taken an iron will, yet he knew, as the world knew, that history was in the balance.

Following his vote he returned home. He'd grimace as he walked without complaining about the pain. Church ladies and relatives kept him company during the rest of the day as sadness gripped his heart and pain racked his body, so much so that sometimes he walked around his house as loose as a straw puppet held upright by strings.

When the drama of election night began to crest, and tears had gushed—and a nation, seemingly against the odds of history, had miraculously leapt over a piece of the mountaintop and elected the first black man president of the United States—Eugene Allen was sitting in his favorite chair, inches from where Helene used to sit. He had a lovely little smile upon his cinnamon-colored face.

My story, about the history of blacks in the White House, from the kitchen to the West Wing, and about Eugene and Helene Allen, and about the civil rights movement and all those prayers for Barack Obama, was titled "A Butler Well Served by This Election." It appeared on the front page of the *Washington Post* on November 7, 2008, three days after the election—and on the very day that Helene Allen was buried.

The election had, indeed, well served all those who had endured brutal segregation and were still alive: those who had been beaten during the sit-ins in North Carolina, who had marched over the

Edmund Pettus Bridge in Alabama, who had started off on civil rights marches and been thrown inside the notorious Parchman Penitentiary in Mississippi. All those alive who remembered the signs WHITE, COLORED. Even in a world of speed, of gadgetry gone amok, of impersonal machinery, this was epic. This was history that welcomed every other historic milestone into this moment. People everywhere reached for comparisons, but because this was America, once a land rife with Klansmen and lynchings and second-class citizenship emblazoned in the laws, there really were no comparisons. And yet, an old man who had fulfilled his civic responsibilities that morning sat alone in an easy chair in Northwest Washington, and the leap in his life felt epic as well. From plantation to ballot slip and a vote for Barack Obama.

After publication of the story, the letters written to me and Eugene Allen came from all corners of America as well as from around the world. The story had been picked up and reprinted in a great many newspapers. We both were surprised and touched. Some evenings, after work, I'd tote a bagful of the letters through the winter darkness over to his home. Here he is at the door, a little stooped, the arms at a perpetual crooked angle, offering a little smile. Not long after my arrival this evening, and after our unfolding chitchat—about the extreme cold outside, about the letter that had arrived from outgoing president George W. Bush and Laura Bush about the loss of Helene—he puts on his bifocals as I hand him some of the letters I've pulled from my shoulder bag. He delicately opens and starts reading one after the other.

From Diana Glenn:

What a touching story. Although I don't have contacts, I am sure you do. I certainly hope that Eugene Allen is invited to dinner in the White House with President Obama. Your story was picked up by the Bend Bulletin *in Bend, Oregon.*

From Jason Whitely:

My best to Mr. Allen and his family who struggle with great loss at such a proud and fascinating turning point in history.

From Kimberly Randolph:

Haven't I cried every day this week, and here I am wiping my eyes again . . . Who's going to take care of Gene now that Helene's gone? Gene definitely should be there at the White House on Jan. 20, 2009.

From Phyllis C. McLaughlin:

How sad that his wife died before she could vote in this historic election . . . What a wonderful couple. My heart really goes out to him.

From Martin Cain:

Thank you for your story about Mr. Allen and his amazing career . . . I am a 58 [year old] white male . . . My vote was going to be cast for McCain. On my drive to the polling place, I started thinking about America's history and the moment that was quite possibly at hand for the American people—not just black Americans, but all Americans. I walked in and voted for Obama. I think that on an intellectual level I can understand the excitement over the significance of the Obama election. I know that I can never understand it on an emotional level . . . I cried when I realized that Helene had died before the election. Please extend my sincere condolences to Mr. Allen and his family.

There were more letters—from Australia, from Japan—and far too many to read in one sitting. "My goodness," the butler said, letting out a little whoop of laughter. "They're awfully nice."

"Would you like some tea? Some coffee?" Maybe he'd never get over the urge to serve. But I said no because I couldn't bear to see him rise, grimacing, and amble off into the kitchen. Sometimes we'd just sit, in silence, *The Price Is Right* droning on the television, the episodes playing back to back yet again. I know he missed Helene. I wondered, that night, and even on other nights, if I were somewhat to blame for

Helene's leaving this earth, if my questions during the interview had exhausted her, stressed her, had caused a slowing of her heart until it just stopped. Then I'd remind myself that her son had told me how she had expressed to him how happy she was feeling before she ascended the stairs for what would be her last night of life on earth—happy that the story of Eugene Allen would finally be written.

Standing outside, on the porch, in the winter darkness, I'd wait until I heard the deadbolt lock click from inside. Then the butler would pull back the curtain and wave good-bye.

My man Godfrey.

My man Eugene.

Allen once spoke of Nixon pacing the corridors of the White House, deliberating inner office turmoil and his distrust of the press. In a public setting, an American president always appears confident, bold, and assured. The public sees them surrounded by the trappings of power. Didn't Kennedy himself look vibrant at Cape Canaveral, in those cool sunglasses and surrounded by his space dreams? There was the ageless Ronald Reagan seen chopping wood with an axe in that rustic California setting, an image that seemed to speak of virility and power. If a man's home, however, is his castle, what is the White House in which he dwells? The front door hardly keeps nightmares or bad tidings away. Is it also, at times, a bewildering chamber where the imagination can drift and wander? It is quite easy to imagine Eugene

Allen bidding me farewell, turning from the door, and descending into his basement, where it is all gathered, where his world remains frozen in time, like a newsreel stopped two floors beneath his Helene-less bedroom. The pictures of him and Ike, of him and boxing champs inside the White House, of him and Mamie Eisenhower, of him snapping that picture of Daddy King, daddy to the civil rights leader. Ruminating, like some of the presidents he served, walking in the quiet dreamscape of a late night to fortify himself for the days ahead, to remember some of the glory of what had gone on before. At home, the president of his own life.

Some weeks later I returned to share news: the transition team of President-elect Obama would be sending a VIP invitation for Eugene Allen to attend the inauguration. There was more news: Hollywood movie producers had begun calling. There was talk of a desire to do a movie about his life. "Well, I'll be doggone," he said. He smiled through pain. All his life he had worked on his feet. Now the ailments seemed to be everywhere inside his body—shoulders, hips, calves. A VIP invitation and Hollywood calling: I wondered how much any of it really meant to him. There was no one in the house to remind him to take his pills. There was no one—on those evenings he was in the mood—for whom to set out the fine china and light a candle. The way he used to do in the White House. The way he used to do for Helene. I could have shared the news over the phone, but I had grown fond of him by then. As I walked away from the home of Eugene Allen on that evening, I was reminded of my own neighborhood in Columbus, Ohio. The neighborhoods shared similarities: tidy streets, solidly built homes, yards with fences and rows of hedges. Working-class neighborhoods. When I finished college, I had returned to reside with my grandparents and not my mother. Old people charm me. Maybe the distance from this street in Washington to my own neighborhood in Columbus was not that great at all.

———

DURING THE HISTORIC campaign of Barack Obama in 2008, stories of America's racial history were constantly unspooling in daily and weekly publications: Michelle Obama's enslaved forebears had been traced to a plantation in South Carolina. The White House—the residence to which Barack Obama was trying to gain entrance—had actually been physically built with the labor of slaves. How black was Obama? Many denizens of the urban hair salons would point to his father's being from Africa itself—the motherland. His story was so mesmerizing, so bewilderingly fascinating, that it was beyond irony. But the world of 1600 Pennsylvania Avenue had always been pulled into the nation's racial agonies.

Throughout history blacks have looked to the White House for help and leadership in the march toward equality.

In 1863 President Lincoln, utilizing his ferocious political acumen, had ingeniously forced Congress into adopting the Thirteenth Amendment to abolish slavery. Chains fell from both ankles and wrists. But he paid with his life. (The momentous legislative victory to abolish slavery was the subject of *Lincoln,* a 2012 Steven Spielberg film. Spielberg, incidentally, had been one of the directors initially interested in telling the Eugene Allen story.) Reconstruction, in the aftermath of Lincoln's assassination, sought to expand black aspirations. In 1866 Frederick Douglass—onetime slave and among the most famous abolitionists of his time—made it to the White House to plead with President Andrew Johnson about black voting rights. Johnson allowed that he had no political capital to gain from fighting for blacks to have the right to vote. Douglass secured another White House invitation in 1877. On this occasion there wasn't even the pretense of politics: President Rutherford B. Hayes had engaged Douglass to serve as master of ceremonies for a festive evening of entertainment.

On October 16, 1901, a Negro butler at the White House was told that President Theodore Roosevelt would be having an evening guest. Just before the appointed time, the butler dutifully set the table. The guest, alone, arrived under the cover of darkness—and in secret. It was Booker T. Washington, the famed educator, also born into slavery. A

Negro had never before dined at the White House. His mere presence made the butler both curious and nervous. Lynchings were still common in the Maryland countryside, a scant distance from the White House itself. According to later accounts, Washington and Roosevelt primarily talked about southern politics and strife in that region. The next morning a smallish item about the dinner appeared on newswires. In short order, all hell, indeed, broke loose. Southerners excoriated Roosevelt for having invited Washington to dine at the White House. The *Memphis Scimitar* was among the first to unleash its invective: "The most damnable outrage which has ever been perpetrated by any citizen of the United States was committed yesterday by the President, when he invited a nigger to dine with him at the White House." It went on: "It is only recently that President Roosevelt boasted that his mother was a Southern woman, and that he is half Southern by reason of that fact. By inviting a nigger to his table he pays his mother small duty . . ."

There were, to be sure, shards of light amid the darkness that sometimes flowed from the White House when it came to black Americans. In 1939—the year a natty-dressing Eugene Allen was plotting to get out of rural Virginia for better job opportunities—the Daughters of the American Revolution, who controlled bookings to Constitution Hall, refused to allow opera singer Marian Anderson to sing on that stage because of their segregation policy. First Lady Eleanor Roosevelt, a member of the DAR, abruptly quit. Her stance gained wide and appreciative coverage in the Negro press. More significant, she arranged for Anderson to perform on the steps of the Lincoln Memorial on Easter Sunday 1939.

By contrast, First Lady Bess Truman, who hailed from the border state of Missouri, was a devoted member of the DAR. When the DAR refused to allow Hazel Scott—a noted pianist and wife of Harlem congressman Adam Clayton Powell Jr.—an engagement in 1945 at Constitution Hall, another war of words erupted. Powell pleaded with President Truman to do something. Truman said he could not, offering that the DAR was a private organization and he intended to stay out of its business. Bess Truman steadfastly refused to quit the DAR. Powell—who could be dangerously quick with a quip—referred to First Lady Bess Truman as "the last lady of the land." President Truman, inside the White House, erupted over Powell's disparaging remark and referred to Powell as "that damn nigger preacher." The public weighed in; letters poured into the White House. One missive addressed to Bess Truman spotlighted the plight of blacks in battle: "In light of their sacrifice it is a shocking fact to realize that you refused yesterday to give up a cup of tea and a box of cookies to support the thesis for which they died." There were those who thought Powell had embarrassed the White House. "On the other hand, Powell has certainly seized a dramatic way to strike at prejudice," a Missouri newspaper noted, "and like Cato (who had warned of the cracking of the Roman empire) is serving the nation by calling attention to danger."

Among the first tasks Eugene Allen was given inside the White House kitchen when he was hired as a pantry man was washing the cups and saucers from which President Truman and Bess Truman drank their daily tea.

———

THE WHITE HOUSE butlers who happened to be Negro operated in a private world inside the White House. It must have been a great responsibility—perhaps somewhat of a burden—for them to carry all those secrets with them through the years. Wives and relatives constantly needled them about what went on inside 1600 Pennsylvania Avenue: Were there secret escape tunnels in the White House? Was Jackie Kennedy nice—or snobbish? Did LBJ use the word "niggers"? (By all accounts, the greatest president on civil rights since Lincoln did use that word.)

Once outside the White House, there was another private world that awaited these butlers. That world was the one populated by ambassadors, famous actors, publishing tycoons, and the moneyed gentry who lived up and down the East Coast. They were families in Washington, New York City, in Hartford, Connecticut, and in Newport, Rhode Island; they were the swells who summered out on Long Island. They held soirees and lavish parties for their friends flying in from the West Coast, and they often turned to White House butlers to work those parties.

These Negro butlers—and a good many of them had been trained by Eugene Allen himself—were in such demand during the 1940s, 1950s, and 1960s that they formed the Private Butler Membership Club. They were known for their punctiliousness and their professionalism, which made them prized recruits for these social affairs. "Those men were jazz and bebop cats who had their own swagger and suited up at night to serve world leaders as the invisible ones," recalls Daphne Muse, whose father, Fletcher Muse Sr., and uncle, George Allen Muse, were members of the Private Butler Membership Club. Both men had been hired as contract butlers at the White House, where they first met Eugene Allen. "It was a tight circle of men," adds Muse. When they ventured to out-of-town assignments, the butlers would often arrive back home laden with bags of delicacies. "A twenty-five-pound bag of blue crab meat would be considered leftovers," says Muse. But it was their discretion that some prized above all else. Muse chuckles at one particular memory of a certain butler who told her, late in his life, what went on at an out-of-town private function: sex, and plenty of it. The affair turned out to be an orgy, and the butler was forced to tiptoe—tray in hand—around the gyrating bodies.

———

IN LOOKING BACK over my own writing life, it seems now that Eugene Allen was a kind of capstone to all those fascinating figures I had interviewed in years past who had a link to turmoil inside the White House.

Scenes from this writer's life:

It's 1986 and I'm sitting in a motel room on the edge of Little Rock, Arkansas, with a frail man launching a campaign for Arkansas governor. He is not just any man; he is Orval Faubus, the governor of Arkansas during the 1957 Little Rock school crisis. He's another old pol who can't let go. He has been talking about redemption of late, but the blacks in the state—and many whites, it must be stated—just rolled their eyes at him. He's the very governor who had forced the Eisenhower administration to call out federal troops to ensure the safety of the nine Negro students back in 1957. He seems so courteous, and he does not wish to really talk about the past, though he does offer that, in 1957, he was only trying to uphold states' rights.

It's 1991 and I'm in a Harlem apartment with E. Frederick Morrow. He was the first black hired—in 1955—in an executive position at the White House. He is seated on a sofa, a proud man, a Bowdoin College graduate. He operated in a society before there was any modern civil rights legislation. The epithets he heard! There were even blacks who made fun of him for working in a Republican administration.

It's 1992 and I'm sitting in the home of Louis Martin, the Democratic

The young Eugene, standing center, newly arrived in Washington, DC, during the Great Depression.

Fifteen-year-old Helene dreaming of leaving her southern childhood and making her way to the nation's capital.

She said yes!

Eugene and Helene at home with son, Charles, 1948.

Sitting on the left is the beautiful and young Helene.

Eugene Allen, left, in his first year on the job with a fellow butler, 1952.

A well-dressed butler inside the Truman White House.

Allen serving guests on the White House lawn during the Eisenhower years.

Eugene Allen, the man in the background.

In the White House pantry,
where it all began.

The displays always had a look of opulence. Allen stands at center alongside the chef.

Always, the flowers were in bloom.

The hours were long, but he never complained and never missed a day of work in thirty-four years.

A little two-step inside the White House.

The day after the Kennedy assassination, Eugene Allen tries to lift White House spirits by having an impromptu party for the Kennedy children and their friends.

Eugene Allen turns photographer to snap a picture of Martin Luther King Sr., known in the movement as Daddy King.

Stars like Peter Lawford would often send Eugene Allen autographed pictures following their visit to the White House.

Life inside the LBJ White House as the sixties near an end.

Charles Allen in Vietnam. Back in America, his father, Eugene Allen, is busy serving LBJ, who sent the Allens' only son to war.

The King of Pop visits the White House; Eugene Allen in rear at right.

Eugene Allen was the first butler in the history of the White House to be invited to a state dinner.

In 1986, West German chancellor Helmut Kohl greets Eugene Allen. Not a White House butler on this night, but a White House special guest.

The Allens were longtime watchers of *The Price Is Right*.

In nearly half a century of serving others, a moment of personal relaxation.

On January 20, 2009, Eugene Allen braved the frigid temperatures in Washington, DC, to finish the final lap of his amazing journey—the historic inauguration of Barack Obama, the nation's first black president, who had invited him.

operative whose work on behalf of black hopes and ambitions stretches back to the Franklin D. Roosevelt administration. It was Martin who had been the principal organizer of the one-hundredth-anniversary celebration of the Emancipation Proclamation in 1963 at the White House during the Kennedy administration. The more he talks about those times—fighting for civil rights, getting Negroes like Martin Luther King Jr. and A. Philip Randolph into the White House for visits—the more he dabs at his tears with the white handkerchief in his hand. The memories of the battles still overwhelm him.

I'm sitting—it's 1993—with an old wheezing man, George Wallace, who's in a wheelchair in his office in Montgomery, Alabama. At one point in American history Alabama's Governor Wallace represented the reason blacks had fled the South: he was the governor who stood in the door at the University of Alabama and said blacks would never be admitted to the school. His choice of words—"segregation now, segregation tomorrow, segregation forever"—would become a rallying cry for segregationists and Klansmen. In 1972 a deranged man shot George Wallace while he was on the campaign trail. That day in Montgomery he tells me stories of all the black friends he now has, of all those who have forgiven him.

Another day—it's 2002—the sun is starting to set, and I'm leaning on a car outside a broken-down auto body shop in Jackson, Mississippi. James Meredith, who integrated Ole Miss in 1962, is talking about poverty, and black folk and white folk, and Mississippi, and being fearless, and history. He's forty years removed from that day that riveted a nation and sparked riots on the campus. He tells me how much he loves the state of Mississippi, where mobs once thought him the embodiment of every black person trying to strive ahead.

I'd come to spend time with all these men as a writer, a journalist and biographer chasing stories throughout America's main roads and back roads. At certain moments in history, all of them caused some kind of emotion, or tumult, to engulf the White House over the issue of blacks and equal rights. And during all those moments, through years and years—bullets and fires and assassinations upon the land—an unknown butler by the name of Eugene Allen was inside the White House. He saw and heard the now historic names, all the images. He certainly would have heard some of the phone calls, eyed some of the men arriving at the White House to see the president to talk about Little Rock, or Oxford, Mississippi. Or Birmingham. He had to take it in, decipher it, process it emotionally. He was, yes, the man with the tray, the medicine, the tea, the bowl of soup; he was the butler who fetched the president's straw hat, the president's wingtips. But he was also a black man. And he saw the ground shifting from up close.

Some nights, when he arrived home from the White House, alighting from his car on Otis Place, after yet another cataclysmic event revolving around black Americans and their epochal struggle for freedom that had overtaken the television screens, Eugene Allen's neighbors would want to rush from their porches and plead with him for information. Anything, dammit, just any tidbit, any morsel of information. But Helene had trained these neighbors well over the years—a perceptible nod, a few pointed words in the grocery store aisle: Eugene couldn't talk; he had to be discreet; he was no one's gossip. Of course that didn't necessarily stop Helene herself from asking questions. Little Charles would hear them whispering at the kitchen table. He'd be playing with his toys in the living room. He'd hear low-pitched talk about his father's workday at the White House. Then, soon as he'd amble into the kitchen, such talk ceased. And the conversation turned to ho-hum things rather than the doings at the White House, where the leader of the free world lived.

How does a man, a butler, a Negro butler in the era of segregation, keep it all inside? Keep gliding about the premises when so much happening around him affects his own life and that of his family? Discretion plays an important role for sure, as does a love of country.

I'm reminded of the line uttered in *The Butler* by Martin Luther King Jr. himself: "Young brother, the black domestic plays an important role in our history." He seems to be talking about pride, and honor of job, and their contribution to the slow march forward.

IT WAS BITTERLY cold—temperatures would hover throughout the day between ten and twenty degrees—on the morning of January 20, 2009, in Washington. At 6:30 a.m. I stood inside the home of Eugene Allen. We would be going together to the inauguration of the nation's first black president. Watching the onetime butler descend the stairs— those tiny grimaces creasing his face again—I wondered if we had made a mistake. I now wasn't so sure he could make it; I thought the long day ahead would be too much. During my recent visits, Eugene Allen had started wrapping his arm around me, giving a tight hug. It touched me. He did so upon reaching the bottom of the stairs, even as I could hear the air coming up through his lungs. When I expressed concern about how he felt, he told me not to worry. "I'll be okay," he said, standing near the framed picture of President and Nancy Reagan and Helene that hung in the living room. I helped him into his long gray wool overcoat. He donned a Sinatra fedora. His son, Charles, was outside revving up the engine, letting the heat ooze throughout the insides of the Cadillac. We rode the car to a subway station and boarded the train. We knew there'd be a lengthy walk once we reached the final train stop. The train was packed but amazingly orderly. No one wished—not on this day—to cause any kind of disruption or disturbance. Charles held one arm of his father, I held the other.

When we emerged from the train station, it was a scene reminiscent of *The Day of the Locust,* with people far as the eye could see. The crowd would surge to more than two million people. Almost immediately, Eugene Allen needed to sit down. He was exhausted. We found a cement barrier and he caught his breath. His son rewrapped the scarf, tighter, around his father's neck. We started making our way to our seating area, up streets crowded with police officers on horseback and thousands upon thousands of pedestrians. A third of a mile into the walk, I strongly suggested we turn back and find a taxi. We needed to get Eugene Allen home; he was breathing heavily. And I felt like a fool for having him out in this brutally cold weather. But then Eugene Allen turned to me and said, "Just get me out of the cold for a spell. I need to get someplace warm. Then we'll keep going." We found a police substation. I was freezing. Charles was freezing. And the butler was freezing. We all sat sipping hot chocolate. After twenty minutes, with Eugene Allen again saying he had no intention of turning back, we continued on our way.

We finally reached the VIP section. A Marine guard greeted Eugene Allen and escorted us to our cold, metallic seats, a cold wind whipping all around us. We could see the area in the distance where the president would take the oath of office. We could see Aretha Franklin's huge and colorful hat atop her head. Eugene Allen sat looking around, taking it all in. He said he knew how much Helene would have loved being here. A parade of figures started strolling and taking their seats in an area above us on the Capitol rotunda steps. Many were figures the butler had served over the years. "There's Jimmy Carter," he said. "He's looking good, too. Took me with him over to Camp David once. When he came into the dining room there—they had given me the day off when I went with them there—he pointed to an empty seat and said to me, 'Who sitting here, Gene?' And I said, 'No one, Mr. President.' And he said, 'Good, I'll sit right here by Gene.'"

President-elect Barack Obama strolled into view. Clearly overjoyed, the butler said, "I'm telling you, it's something to see. Seeing him standing there—well, it's been worth it all."

———

WORTH IT ALL? Maybe he was talking about the long trek from a Virginia plantation, the verbal abuse he was subjected to while working in a country club; maybe he was talking about all the dishes he had washed in his life, all the moonless nights he had alighted from the White House on his trek home, bone weary. Maybe he was talking about the 1960s, when the kids with the afros in his neighborhood, the ones wearing those "Black Power" buttons, wondered why in the world he was still working over at the White House—as a butler.

At ceremony's end—with history washing over everyone in attendance—Eugene Allen rose, he tightened his gloves, and we all headed back home. More than a few people recognized him from the story that had been written about him just after the election. They shook his hand.

That afternoon, back home, sitting in his easy chair, Eugene Allen fell asleep. The television had been playing *The Price Is Right*.

In the second week of March 2010 I hopped aboard a city bus in Washington, DC, and rode over to Providence Hospital. Charles had phoned and told me his father had been admitted two days earlier with some respiratory and hip problems. He was lying in bed, though wide awake, when I arrived. "The nurses take good care of me," he said. "They think I'm famous." One of the nurses had remembered the articles written about him; soon word got around the hospital, and doctors and nurses dropped by to meet him. They'd mention how amazing it was he had worked all those years at the White House. When Allen fell asleep that day, Charles and I strolled the hallways, worried. The old man appeared to be weakening. Still, he rallied in the days ahead and was released. The return home didn't last long. He told Charles one day he was feeling terrible. He was admitted to Washington Adventist Hospital, where, on March 31, 2010, Eugene Allen, butler to eight presidents, took his last labored breath.

It had been a mere sixteen months earlier that I had first met Eugene Allen and his wife, Helene, that he had first escorted me down into a darkened basement that held such treasures from a life inside the White House. A day after he died, his obituary appeared in newspapers all around America. He received lovely tributes on the national news telecasts. "Eugene Allen has died," Brian Williams said on *NBC Nightly News,* as pictures of Allen revolved on a screen. "Few Americans will ever get to see as much history as he did, and only a handful have ever been this close to power." There was swelling music. Williams continued, "He served the most powerful and most famous people in the world. And after hours a lot of presidents treated him as their friend." His death was noted around the world as well. The *Independent* of London described Eugene Allen as "a discreet stage hand who for three decades helped keep the show running in the most important political theatre of all." The obituaries all made mention that he had voted for Barack Obama amid the sadness of losing his wife on Election Eve.

SEVERAL HUNDRED PEOPLE strolled into the Greater First Baptist Church in Washington on April 8, 2010, to bid Eugene Allen farewell. The long line of men along the back row of the church were Secret Service agents. A few had gotten to know Allen during gatherings at the White House after he retired. Most had just come out of respect. There were rows of flowers near his casket. There were aging butlers and maids seated in the pews. Delores Moaney, who had worked at the White House during the Eisenhower years, recalled: "He was such a charming man. I had worked as a maid with the Eisenhower family in New York. When I got to the White House, I met Gene. You'd notice his smile right away." The first female usher at the White House was Nancy Mitchell. She got the position in 1980. Some days inside the White House she was just a jangle of nerves, worrying she might do something wrong. "Gene—he told me to call him Gene, but I never could—calmed me down. He'd come and get me and say, 'Nancy, let's go get some lunch.' And he had already set up a lovely place setting for me and him. He may have been the best man I ever met."

President Obama sent over a letter. It was read by the chief White House usher, Rear Admiral Stephen W. Rochon: "His life represents an important part of the American story," the president's letter said of Eugene Allen. It went on to cite the butler for his decades of service to the country and his "abiding patriotism."

The Reverend Winston C. Ridley talked about Allen and the sweep of history—the world wars away from our shores, the wars over equality inside our own borders. "Now, it's true that some tried to stigmatize his job, that of butler. But Eugene Allen raised it to a level of excellence."

There were several musical numbers by the choir, among them "Jesus on the Main Line" and "Oh Mary Don't You Weep."

I caught a glimpse of the suit the butler lay in before they closed his casket. It was a formal, gray evening suit. He had on white gloves, just like the elegant ones he sometimes wore at 1600 Pennsylvania Avenue when he was serving the high and mighty. Flowers adorned the casket. One card pinned to a bouquet of red roses read "President Obama and Michelle Obama." The aging butlers and maids who had known Allen through the years began making their way slowly out of the church. Outside it was crisp and bright.

It was, as President Obama said, quite an American story: a young man who had fled a southern plantation, who had made his way to the nation's capital, who had witnessed the tumult and glory of change from a unique position, who had crossed from one century to the next while working for eight presidents. And who had also seen the once unimaginable: the swearing in of a black president.

There was even a bit more. In late 2012 a local organization put Eugene's home on a historic walking tour map of Washington. It was now known as "The Eugene Allen Residence." A movie had also been completed about his life, and among its stars were Forest Whitaker and Oprah Winfrey (playing characters inspired by Eugene and Helene), Jane Fonda, Vanessa Redgrave, Robin Williams, David Oyelowo, and Cuba Gooding Jr. The movie told the story of the whole modern civil rights movement, from the vantage point of a White House butler.

Why, Eugene Allen would have some mighty interesting stories to tell Helene.

MOVING IMAGE

I N THE SUMMER OF 2012, more than three dozen large trucks and trailers rolled through the narrow streets of New Orleans carrying all manner of film equipment. There was equipment to make it rain on a movie set when a scene called for rain. There were klieg lights powerful enough that, even at midnight, they could make it seem from inside a room as if it were daylight beyond the windows. The drivers parked in a huge lot, known as "base camp." It would be the daily staging area over the next thirty-seven days for the stars, producers, and director of *The Butler,* a major motion picture to be directed by Oscar nominee Lee Daniels. The production office had been set up and staffed, weeks earlier, on Prytania Street. The actors and actresses who had signed on to the project had raised interest on both sides of the Atlantic. It was quite a starry cast, an eclectic assemblage of Oscar winners and nominees. Among them were Forest Whitaker, Oprah Winfrey, Jane Fonda, Robin Williams, Cuba

Gooding Jr., David Oyelowo, Mariah Carey, Vanessa Redgrave, and Terrence Howard.

When I first saw the rows and rows of trucks and trailers at base camp, I imagined that several movie productions must be headquartered there. "Nope, it's all for *The Butler*," Evan Arnold, a production aide, told me. Evan suggested I walk along the spaces that separated the rows of trucks; he told me to make sure I looked at the writing on the side of each truck. The movie's title, *The Butler*—based on an article I had written—appeared on the side of those trucks. We were in New Orleans and Evan was allowing a "Welcome to Hollywood" grin. It was quite a scene to take in.

Movies are notoriously difficult to mount and get made no matter the subject. Turning the story of a black man who served as a White House butler for more than thirty years into a motion picture came with its own set of huge challenges, and it mirrors the story I hope to tell here, a look at blacks in cinema. It is a narrative that can often be aligned—when viewing it through a historical lens—with the struggle for equal rights. And in many ways, that cinematic struggle began, like a part of Eugene Allen's life covered in this movie, also in the White House.

———

IT WAS IN 1914 when film director D. W. Griffith set about making a film based on *The Clansman,* a novel written by Thomas Dixon. The novel was a nasty piece of work; Dixon was an avowed racist, and his book featured nearly every imaginable stereotype heaped upon blacks at the time. The novel was set in the aftermath of the Civil War, during Reconstruction, and told of blacks pillaging, lunging after defenseless white women, engaging in corruption, and finally being rooted from their savagery by the "heroic" Klan. Griffith, the filmmaker—who was born in Kentucky and still harbored resentment that his father had been a defeated Confederate soldier—salivated over the novel's brew.

A little more than a year after filming began, Griffith's movie, titled *The Birth of a Nation,* opened in Los Angeles. Moviegoers sat and appeared amazed; their eyes glazed over. By movie's end, those in their seats believed they had just watched an epic. The prolonged applause was deafening. Griffith quieted rumors that he himself was in attendance when he appeared on stage, an aging gnome of a man. "He stepped out a few feet from the left, a small, almost frail figure lost in the enormousness of this great proscenium arch," noted an account. "He did not bow or raise his hands or do anything but just stood there and let wave after wave of cheers and applause wash over him like a great wave breaking over a rock."

Filmgoing at the time was relatively new, and this particular film ignited nationwide interest and abundant ticket sales. The news of the movie's charged reception raced around the country via telegrams, newspaper reports, and movie magazines. It also swelled the ranks of the Ku Klux Klan, whose members saw the movie as nothing less than emblematic of their own sentiments and beliefs. The movie, however, alarmed NAACP officials, who organized boycotts. Some cities, fearing riots, refused to show it. Joel Spingarn, an NAACP official, told that organization's board that *The Birth of a Nation* had helped to "unloosen the energy and to stimulate the support of the colored people of this country as this attack [was] on their character and their place in history." Editorialists from Negro publications castigated the movie, then watched their backs as they departed their offices, fearing attacks.

Dixon, the novelist, had reached out to President Woodrow Wilson, bragging to him about the movie's popularity. He found in Wilson, also a southerner, a receptive audience. Wilson decided to show it at the White House, making it the first movie to be screened there. Wilson watched with eyes widening. A learned man who had been educated at Princeton, the first president to possess a PhD, he was, nonetheless, absolutely uncritical of the cinematic vision before him. As the credits rolled, he gleefully claimed he had never seen anything like it. "It is like writing history with lightning," he said. "And my only regret is that it is all so terribly true."

Thus, a movie that pilloried black Americans had been praised at the White House itself by the president of the United States. Cinema for and about blacks as an art form was truly light-years away.

Black Americans, well aware of the imagery on the big screen, made efforts in the early twentieth century to effect their own cinematic history. In 1915 George and Nobel Johnson formed the Lincoln Motion Picture Company. They aimed to tell stories about black Americans and to counter the popularity of *The Birth of a Nation* and other filmed treatments such as *Uncle Tom's Cabin, How Rastus Got His Turkey,* and *Coon Town Suffragettes.* But the filmmakers were done in by disease: the spread of influenza across the country kept theatergoers away and their business was forced to shutter.

Oscar Micheaux was close behind the Johnson brothers. A son of former slaves, he lifted himself up into the world of show business. Micheaux went from shoeshine stand owner to Pullman porter on trains, then landowner in the American West. He started writing, newspaper articles at first, then autobiographical novels, including one entitled *The Conquest: The Story of a Negro Pioneer.* He had enough chutzpah to sell the book door to door. But Micheaux also wanted to make movies, and when no one would give him a deal to turn one of his novels, *The Homesteader,* into a picture, he decided to direct and produce it himself. A quick thinker, he vowed to recruit investors, telling them that black-oriented movies could turn a profit. (Black filmmakers today, Lee Daniels among them, often adopt the same strategy.) In an effort to fill seats in those theaters, Micheaux wrote his own ads: "Every Race man and woman should cast aside their skepticism regarding the Negro's ability as a motion picture star, and go."

Throughout the 1920s Oscar Micheaux was the most prolific

black filmmaker in the country, though it was a fraternity so thin as to be mostly invisible. He showed no hesitancy in courting controversy, making movies about lynchings, miscegenation, and skulduggery in the Negro church. Recognized as someone who had an eye for scouting unknown talent, he promoted Lorenzo Tucker as "the black Valentino" and gave Paul Robeson his first film role in 1925 in Micheaux's *Body and Soul*. Against a backdrop of inequality and desperate times—though he seemed blessed with heaps of hubris—it's a wonder Micheaux even got his more than forty films made. They were largely devoid of stereotype, though they were rarely mistaken for art; it was Micheaux's grit that was heroic.

Other movies of the era could not escape the dagger of stereotype when it came to blacks. Black women were seen as either housemaids or taciturn nannies. A good many family acts managed to make it on screen. In 1933 an aging vaudevillian by the name of Will Mastin hustled one of his little dancers over to a soundstage in Brooklyn. The little dancer, Sammy Davis Jr., had gotten the lead role in the movie *Rufus Jones for President*. (Back to the White House!) In the short, which also featured Ethel Waters, the little child dreams of being president. The dreamscape unfolds and the cinemagoer sees it all: The cute child is seen prancing about, a chorus of singers and dancers around him, uttering jokes about watermelons and pork chops being given away freely. There is a sign near a doorway in the dream: "VOTE HERE FOR RUFUS

JONES—Two Pork Chops Every Time You Vote." When the child Rufus walks by a Senate door, he sees another sign: CHECK YOUR RAZORS. In the dream the child becomes the president. Of course, in the dream, he has a vice president. As the movie shows, the vice president is his "mammy"! In real life, removed from a dream, stage appearances could be just as wicked for little Sammy Davis Jr. Sometimes, on stage, he wore blackface. Thus he was a black child, in whiteface, pretending to be a white man in blackface—all for the laughter of white film audiences.

Even the grown-up black actors who found occasional film work in the 1940s—Lena Horne, Dorothy Dandridge, Eddie "Rochester" Anderson—had to endure humiliating slights from which some never recovered. Though lighter-skinned black women such as Horne appeared more palatable to white film audiences, they had no easy time of it. In 1954 Dorothy Dandridge, for her performance in *Carmen Jones,* became the first black woman to garner a best actress Oscar nomination. But the acclaim seemed just a torturous tease: despite the recognition, the studios did not send her challenging scripts, nor did white male actors lobby for her to appear alongside them. She eventually vanished from the movie screen, suffering from depression and an overdependence on pills. She died broke in 1965. Lena Horne seemed to weather her relationship with Hollywood better than Dandridge simply because, for a while, she was nowhere in Hollywood to be found (though she did return to the big screen in 1969). She was blacklisted from both movies and television work during the fifties. Not a soul in Hollywood challenged Horne's banishment, though there were those who pointed to her friendship with activist Paul Robeson as the reason she was shunned.

In a child's mind, the movies do not easily take on deep social significance. The child goes to the movies to be transported and to look for heroes. Writer James Baldwin was no different from any other child who was growing up, watching tall figures on the wide movie screen. "I did not yet know," the great writer would recall about being a twelve-year-old, "that virtually every black community in America contains a movie house, or, sometimes, in those days, an actual theater, called the Lincoln, or the Booker T. Washington, nor did I know why; any more than I knew why The Cotton Club was called The Cotton Club."

Movies are wedded to the American psyche, Baldwin eventually figured out. They are weekly destinations; they are a belief system at work. As an American populace, we go to the movies because they feed our collective imagination. (In my Columbus, Ohio, hometown, the Lincoln Theatre—now wondrously restored—sat right there on Long Street.)

And yet if there was no equality on the streets—as the foot soldiers in the marches and protests of the next decade, those in Birmingham and Selma, the night riders, and the vanguard students sent in to integrate schools illustrated—how could there have been equality in the selection of movies that got made? Positions both in front of and behind the camera seemed closed to blacks, with the exception of movies that starred Harry Belafonte or Sidney Poitier. When the sixties were rounding the corner into view, the whole time line of that epoch, with all its leading men—Martin Luther King Jr., Malcolm X, the Kennedys, Belafonte, Poitier (both of whom were delivering bail money to the protesters across the South), J. Edgar Hoover—something happened up in the Hollywood Hills: the men who ran the movies realized that America was passing them by. The birth of a nation, all right—but with afros and Black Studies programs, civil rights bills and martyrs. It certainly appeared that the Hollywood power brokers had missed a whole movement. Which is why the story of Harry Belafonte and Sidney Poitier—who knew well the struggle of those artists flattened on the roads behind them—is so potent: they broke through before the streets caught fire. Their very presence couldn't help but to nick at the conscience of Hollywood, a place far enough from the murderous small towns of the Deep South as to seem almost in another world.

One can only imagine the amazing and yet lonely trajectory of Sidney Poitier, the first black male movie star in the Hollywood studio system. Poitier honed his skills at the American Negro Theater in Harlem in the 1940s; Harry Belafonte was a fellow acting student and had starring roles in *Carmen Jones* and *Island in the Sun*. Poitier went west, and small movie roles led, in 1958, to a costarring turn in *The Defiant*

Ones opposite Tony Curtis, for which Poitier became the first black man to receive an Oscar nomination for best actor.

Looking back at the American calendar and the role Negroes—the popular term used then—played in society in 1963, one finds more than a few freeze-frame moments to seize upon. That year—Eugene Allen the butler would have been on his job for eleven years—marked the one-hundredth anniversary of the end of American slavery. There was an Emancipation Proclamation event in honor of the occasion at the White House. It did not get much attention in the mainstream media, however, because its lens was focused instead on Birmingham, Alabama, where on September 15, at the Sixteenth Street Baptist Church, Klansmen had set a bomb in reaction against the settlement between the city and the demonstrators who had fought against segregation with protests and boycotts. Four girls, in their Sunday finery, were killed. Martyrs in the struggle, they joined the likes of Emmett Till and Medgar Evers and all the other foot soldiers on the march toward equality. They became sad emblems of the struggle for equal rights in America. Real-life America was just too dangerous for Hollywood's fictions.

In that very year, Sidney Poitier appeared in *Lilies of the Field,* in the role of Homer Smith, playing an itinerant, out-of-work construction worker who helps a group of German nuns build a chapel. The movie opened on the big screen. And for many families—especially Negro families, mine included—it would become an annual staple of family television time, the rare movie with a black lead that had become a rite of cinematic passage. Not unlike *The Wizard of Oz* for so many other households.

The script of *Lilies of the Field* grew out of William E. Barrett's lovely little 127-page novella of the same name. The *New York Times Book Review* described the book, which was published in 1962, as "a contemporary fable." Fable or not, black America now saw a figure on screen who wasn't kowtowing, a man who set his own hours in the world, a man who seemed to roam the earth free and easy. Poitier received an Oscar nomination for best actor for his performance in the movie. His fellow nominees in the category were Albert Finney, Richard Harris, Paul Newman, and Rex Harrison.

Poitier did not dare imagine he could win, and when Anne Bancroft opened the envelope on Oscar night and uttered Poitier's name, it cascaded far beyond the confines of the Santa Monica Auditorium that evening. No one was more surprised than Poitier. This was cinema and history and a breakthrough, but also a balm for the pain in the streets. "It has been a long journey to this moment," Poitier said from the podium, in words that seemed to swoop up an entire race of people. "We black people had done it," he would later write of that evening. "We were capable. We forget sometimes, having to persevere against unspeakable odds, that we are capable of infinitely more than the culture is yet willing to credit to our account."

Did the moment foretell better days ahead for blacks in Hollywood movies? One might fast-forward to this revealing fact: it would not be until 2001 that another black male actor—Denzel Washington, for his magnetic and controversial performance as a corrupt detective in *Training Day*—would be seen holding the Oscar for best actor, almost four decades after Poitier's history-making win. Blacks, who have long been quite vocal about cinema in America, found it hard to believe the long gap between Poitier and Washington had been just misfortune. The gap summoned up overlooked performances from the past, such as Paul Winfield's in 1972 in *Sounder* alongside an equally amazing Cicely Tyson; Ivan Dixon in 1964 in *Nothing But a Man*; James Earl Jones in *The Great White Hope* in 1970. Many in America, especially blacks, seemed to have their fingers crossed especially tight in 1993, hoping Denzel Washington would win for his nominated performance in *Malcolm X*. There were reasons to be hopeful: there had been a long battle waged by filmmaker Spike Lee to get the movie made, and Washington did win a slew of other industry awards for the performance that season. But not the Oscar.

History, however, seemed to be quite sweet the night of Washington's best actor win for *Training Day:* Halle Berry also was named best actress, in a role that was seen as controversial. Portraying a poor southern woman with a husband on death row, she conducts an affair with a white man, and in one scene she strips naked for the camera, a move that prompted many black actresses to question her decision to play a part they thought demeaning.

Even today, the conversation about a lack of richly drawn characters for the gallery of black acting talent still seems to haunt Hollywood, when studies still show a paltry number of blacks filling leading roles in mainstream films. When it comes to directing, the recognition from the Academy for blacks is paltry indeed. In the history of American cinema, only two black directors have ever been nominated for a best directing Oscar: John Singleton, for *Boyz n the Hood,* and Lee Daniels, for *Precious: Based on the Novel "Push" by Sapphire.*

It remains worth noting—to turn the camera back to the 1960s—that Sidney Poitier's historic achievements in film played out in the full gallop of the civil rights movement. The boulders were rolling through the cities and they could not be turned back. The movie camera kept churning, and it would not lose sight of Poitier, which gave blacks a reason to hope and pray when it came to celluloid imagery.

In 1967 Poitier would appear in two much-talked-about films, *Guess Who's Coming to Dinner* and *In the Heat of the Night.* Both made vivid allusion—especially in the impressionable minds of many white moviegoers who lived in a segregated nation—to what it was like to be a black man navigating the shifting social terrain in America during the push to integrate. Poitier the actor felt it up close. Art didn't imitate life. Life reshaped the art.

The plot of *In the Heat of the Night* has Poitier playing a northern police officer who gets stranded in Mississippi. While there, he is talked into helping solve a local murder. Before filming started—verisimilitude be damned—Poitier let director Norman Jewison know he was not going to film in hostile Mississippi. Civil rights workers had been murdered in that state, after all. So the production filmed in Illinois and Tennessee. While the actors were in Tennessee, however, after hearing some rednecks spew epithets, Poitier let it be known he was sleeping with a gun beneath his pillow.

Poitier's other film that year was *Guess Who's Coming to Dinner*. Romance or marriage across the color line was still quite taboo. Even the hint of interracial sex was considered risky in film. So it cannot be underestimated just how novel, even radical, *Guess Who's Coming to Dinner* seemed in 1967. It was a mainstream film, opening up the no-no subject of interracial sex to the American public. The story line revolved around a black man (Poitier) and his girlfriend (played by Katharine Houghton) who must tell her parents (screen legends Spencer Tracy and Katharine Hepburn) that she is marrying a black man—a Negro. By the time the following year's Oscar telecast was shown, the nation had days earlier been delivered the news of Martin Luther King's assassination in Memphis. Anger was now everywhere in urban America. Guess who's coming to the White House? Marchers and protesters got within a block of 1600 Pennsylvania Avenue. (The butlers and maids, Eugene Allen among them, had clear views from the upstairs windows.) That very year the Kerner Commission, ordered to investigate the 1967 riots, had concluded that America was "moving toward two societies, one black, one white—separate and unequal." Hollywood—it was not so subtly reported in the Kerner Report—had helped perpetuate such a society.

Where did that leave Sidney Poitier? There were many, especially figures associated with the black power movement, who thought him too acquiescent to Hollywood for taking on the kind of role he did in *Guess Who's Coming to Dinner*. But Poitier was a touchstone for black America; from White House butlers to factory workers to schoolteachers to sports heroes, he had garnered wide respect. Still, this dynamic of how young and old blacks viewed Poitier created lively conversation from barbershops to dinner tables in the orbit of black America. It is also expressed in an emotional late-1960s scene in *The Butler*. The family—Cecil (modeled on the butler Eugene); Gloria, his wife; and Louis, their son who's rebelling against all that his father stands for—are sitting around the dinner table. Gloria has just told Louis she recently saw Poitier's *In the Heat of the Night*.

LOUIS

Sidney Poitier is the white man's fantasy of what he wants us to be. Well behaved with no sense of his manhood as a sexual being.

CECIL

But his movies have him fighting for equal rights.

LOUIS

Only in a way that is acceptable to the white status quo.

It was impossible for Hollywood to ignore how this sentiment was expressed through the upheaval on the streets. In Los Angeles—the movie capital of the world—the community of Watts erupted in a riot on August 11, 1965. Thirty-four people died. The *Los Angeles Times,* a newspaper both rich and fat at the time, did not have a single black reporter on its full-time staff. They corralled a black messenger to get to the scene and take notes. In Watts, the world could now see, in news-reel footage, the painful woes of inequality that engulfed the country. Filmmakers in the land of sunshine seemed caught in a time warp and spasms of denial. Cinema was right out their front door. Directors were churning out big-budget flops like *Dr. Dolittle* while fires raged not many miles from the movie studios themselves.

What did slip through, though, as a kind of multicultural filmmak-ing moment, was the experimental era of so-called blaxploitation films. Beginning in the 1970s, those films landed in many urban theaters around the country. Nowadays many look dated and seem comically retro. The budgets were indeed low, but the films were imbued with an undercurrent of activism: the male and female stars were anything but subservient or acquiescent. They were aggressive, cool, defiant. They were rebels with causes. On-screen, their afros bobbed in the wind. Their bell-bottoms flared. The dialogue—"whitey," "hey brother," "the man," "dig it"—echoed the patter on the nearest urban street corner. Black moviegoers suddenly had heroes that looked like them, and they flocked to see the movies, among them *The Mack, Foxy Brown, Shaft, Truck Turner, Cleopatra Jones,* and *Super Fly;* the latter had a soundtrack by Curtis Mayfield that would become a classic. The films also provided work for a coterie of black actors who welcomed the opportunity, among them Calvin Lockhart, Ron O'Neal, Bernie Casey, Julius Harris, Sheila Frazier, Richard Pryor, Pam Grier, and Billy Dee Williams.

Then something mighty strange happened in the world of blacks in cinema. The latter half of the 1970s was barren. Blacks actually began to disappear from film. Years rolled by with large swaths of black talent on the sidelines or struggling to get television work. It seemed, in the land of so-called liberal Hollywood, that even the subject of blacks in movies was taboo. The editors of *People* magazine thought otherwise. Their 1982 article "Blacks in Hollywood: Where Have They All Gone?" flung the issue out in the open, where it could not be ignored any longer. The article was scathing and blunt: blacks, it charged, were being "whitelisted" from Hollywood motion pictures. (The term, of course, played on the infamous word "blacklisted" used to describe members of the Hollywood community denied work in the 1950s because of alleged ties to Communist sympathizers.) Those black actors willing to be quoted in the article were incredulous that after the resounding success of the 1977 television miniseries *Roots*—which traced a black family's journey from slavery to freedom in America— they were rewarded with nary a career boost. The Hollywood branch of the NAACP—the very organization that protested the screening of *Birth of a Nation* during President Woodrow Wilson's administration—joined the outcry and also became vocal in bringing attention to the plight of black actors.

In subsequent years, there was only slightly more visibility by black filmmakers and actors in Hollywood. And much of that momentum flowed from the independent film movement, specifically Spike Lee's movies. In 1986 Lee directed *She's Gotta Have It*, followed three years later by *Do the Right Thing*, his seminal movie about simmering race relations in Brooklyn, New York. Lee's films aside, independent films are often, by definition, not profitable in the terms the big studios expect.

THE GREAT AND grand conversations about money and movies hark back to the moguls of the last century. Louis B. Mayer and Samuel Goldwyn both wanted to make profitable pictures. As many in the Hollywood camp are fond of repeating, no business, no show.

When an American movie with a mostly black cast—or even a themed movie where blacks carry the arc of the narrative—comes upon the cinematic landscape, the dialogue heats up. Will the public attend? Will the movie only play in urban areas? There is always the hope for crossover appeal as was the case with Clint Eastwood's *Bird,* which starred *The Butler*'s Forest Whitaker. If subject matter comes into play, slavery is a topic American filmmakers have uniformly shied from. There was Steven Spielberg's *Amistad,* a film about a slave revolt and landmark court case. It was a stirring drama, with gripping performances given by Djimon Hounsou and Anthony Hopkins. Its domestic total gross was $45 million. That is nothing to snicker at, but hardly what a Spielberg film is expected to earn. So many simply concluded the scenes on screen—slaves drowning, shot to death, hogtied—were too tough to sit through. Much the same criticism greeted Quentin Tarantino's *Django Unchained.* Nevertheless, that movie went on to be a robust hit and a prizewinner.

Sometimes a black-themed movie is so unique, so surprising, that the Establishment ignores grubby talk of gross receipts. One such movie was *Daughters of the Dust,* a 1991 movie set in the 1920s in South Carolina. It revolved around a group of women and their musings about migration. The film, directed by Julie Dash, had the sweep of a fever dream. It also did not have a single big-name Hollywood star in it. Aside from its ethereal quality, something else seemed amazing: it was the first movie to gain major distribution in this country that had been directed by a black woman. It set no box office records. In 2004, however, *Daughters of the Dust* was chosen by the Library of Congress to be placed in the National Film Registry for preservation. Art doesn't necessarily get moviegoers into seats, but it can very often be both a noble and an admirable undertaking. Whopping big-budget movies have fallen by the wayside; Dash's small and intimate one will be remembered.

In the category of films that will be remembered but not necessarily profitable is *The Wiz*. It was directed by the great Sidney Lumet and starred the luminous Lena Horne as the Good Witch. It must have seemed like a lovely idea at the time: a black cast reimagining a beloved classic. The movie—both fun to watch and a bit too busy—ultimately suffered from the miscasting of Diana Ross. But blacks thrilled at the sight of a big-budget musical. How many inner-city dreams were hatched from the viewing of that film? We may never know.

Filmmakers are, after all, ultimate gamblers. Throw race into that gamble, and the predictions get a lot trickier. Tyler Perry has legions of admirers, but also those who do not rush to see his comedic work. But there's no denying he's tapped into a vein: movies with predominately black casts that are comedic sending the director-producer go laughing all the way to the bank. Perry has a genius marketing machine: the black church ladies talk of him in gospel-like tones. They bolt for the multiplexes to see his latest after Sunday services. Samuel Goldwyn and

Louis B. Mayer would have loved the Perry formula. A lot of business, a lot of show!

It took George Lucas more than two decades to mount *Red Tails*, his movie about the black Tuskegee Airmen who flew in World War II. He bemoaned that no Hollywood studio wanted to make it, so he financed it himself. It became a modest box office hit, accumulating a $50 million gross. The brave gamblers can certainly win, particularly when measured in terms of both box office rewards and cultural pride. Which begs the question: Why have American filmmakers shied from taking advantage of the greatest civil rights movement in this nation's recent history, that of the 1960s and its oceanic emotions? The territory is fertile and untapped. "I hope *The Butler* causes a movement in that direction," producer Pam Williams told me.

If cinema is a universal language, what does it say about America—and American movies, which are great sources of export—that its movies tend to ignore a whole segment of its populace? Is that not cultural blindness? And yet, bringing attention to the plight hardly seemed to solve the problem.

In writing a story about the 2011 Oscar nominees—for performances in 2010—the estimable *New York Times* film critic Manohla Dargis commended those nominees and pictures for the variety of roles as well as genres. But the nominated films were also, she wrote, "more racially homogenous—more white—than the ten films that were up for best picture in 1940, when Hattie McDaniel became the first black American to win an Oscar for her role as Mammy in 'Gone With the Wind.'" To Dargis, it was painfully obvious that 2010 was "perhaps the whitest year for Hollywood" in decades. For a major film critic to take American movies back to the 1940s when talking about race could only be seen as a rebuke of modern-day filmmaking. The Dargis story appeared in the *Times* on a Sunday, a day of wide circulation, and you could practically hear the gnashing in Hollywood: a black man occupied the Oval Office, yet the movies seemed to be harking back to the kind of "whitelisting" that existed in those mean days of yesteryear. (Interestingly enough, a story in the *New York Times* in June 2013 paid attention to African American–themed movies slated for pending release—one of which was *The Butler*.)

Fortunately, one of those people who had long been concerned about the lack of diversity in American films was Laura Ziskin, a powerful producer in Hollywood. Among her best-known produced works were *Pretty Woman, As Good as It Gets,* and the Spider-Man films. Ziskin was in London when she first read my article "A Butler Well Served by This Election" in the *Washington Post*. She and her producing partner, Pam Williams, tracked me down in a hotel room in Memphis, Tennessee, where I was on assignment.

Ziskin and Williams were immediately drawn to the article as a potential movie and imagined *The Butler* as an epic, a story that would encompass modern civil rights history through the eyes of a White

Forest Whitaker and Oprah Winfrey as Cecil and Gloria Gaines,
the characters inspired by Eugene and Helene Allen.

Director Lee Daniels with Oprah Winfrey as Gloria.

The White House staff, played by Lenny Kravitz,
Forest Whitaker, and Cuba Gooding Jr.

Re-creating the segregation of the 1960s.

David Oyelowo as Gaines's son, Louis,
being arrested for participating in the 1960s sit-ins.

Protesters are hosed down by police.

Producer Pam Williams with Charles Allen (far right) and Rear Admiral Stephen Rochon, the first black chief usher to serve in the White House and the film's White House consultant.

Robin Williams as Dwight D. Eisenhower.

Allen serving Eisenhower and guests during a discussion of civil rights, c. 1955.

Forest Whitaker with Robin Williams.

Camelot comes to the White House: James Marsden and Minka Kelly as the Kennedys.

The butler reads Caroline Kennedy (Chloe Barach) a bedtime story.

Liev Schreiber as Lyndon B. Johnson.

John Cusack as Richard M. Nixon.

The butler and the president had birthdays on the same day. There was much celebration in the Ford White House for both.

A new family moves into the
White House: the Carters.

The butler and two presidents.

First Lady Nancy Reagan was impressed with Eugene Allen's style.

Alan Rickman and Jane Fonda as the Reagans.

Helene Allen on the receiving line, shaking hands with President Reagan. She would become very fond of this photograph.

The butler shares a word with Alan Rickman as President Reagan.

After eight presidents, a farewell send-off for the butler.

The butler greets George H. W. Bush and his wife, Barbara Bush.

Although he never worked in the Clinton White House, Eugene Allen was often invited back. Here he sits next to Hillary Clinton.

Eugene Allen, in front of President George W. Bush, at a butler reunion.

Whitaker in silhouette.

One of the votes that got President Obama to the
White House was cast by Eugene Allen.

House butler. "We sent that article around to potential investors for the film and eventually met with several prominent directors, including one no producer can afford to ignore—Steven Spielberg," Williams remembers. But Spielberg finally admitted he could not squeeze the movie into his schedule of projects already lined up. Other directors were called in for meetings with Ziskin and Williams. None impressed as much as Lee Daniels, who came with a vision, which he laid out over several hours, that nearly brought the two producers to tears.

Lee Daniels, who directed *Precious,* his dynamic and blistering Harlem-set drama about an abused teenager, imagined a movie that would sweep from the White House to the streets of the civil rights movement. It would feature many of the major players from the 1960s; the unsettling footage of Birmingham and Selma and night riders would be brought to life on screen. (The gifted Danny Strong wrote the script.) Such a movie would require a decent-sized budget.

That didn't deter Ziskin, who gritted her teeth and adopted another strategy when she was told by a big studio that she was asking for too much money to mount the film they all wanted to make. If she had to, she'd raise the money independently. In risk-averse Hollywood, that is a common maneuver for many serious filmmakers. Daniels himself was adept at going hat in hand for the sake of art; he had raised much of the money for *Precious* by that method. That movie had taken home two Oscar statuettes, for best supporting actress and adapted screenplay— and had earned him his nomination for best director.

Ziskin and Williams began their new strategy by reaching out to Sheila Johnson, the former cofounder of Black Entertainment Television (BET). The story of a humble, long-serving butler appealed to Johnson: she owns Salamander Hotels and Resorts in Virginia, which employs many domestic workers. "I met Lee at the St. Regis Hotel in New York City," Johnson recalled on the film set one evening. "I was committed before I sat down with Lee. I knew this story had to be told. It is such a layering of history." (It was Johnson's seed money that initially opened the financial gates.)

The quartet—Ziskin, Williams, Daniels, and Johnson—began talking to and bringing in other investors. But as the late winter of 2010 turned to the early months of 2011, it became painfully clear that Ziskin's health—she had been diagnosed years earlier with breast cancer—was worsening. Still, the weaker she grew, the more ferocious she became. She made phone calls late at night and was at it again early in the morning. Between calls, she'd gulp down her medicine, ready to strategize the next move to get her movie made. She'd turn to her daughter, Julia, then to Lee Daniels, who would be visiting, then to Pam Williams, who never seemed to leave her side. After gathering strength from her, they'd each get back on the phone, raising the money needed to make the movie. Laura herself would plead with investors to come to her home, and she told them, as they nibbled on sandwiches, that the story was too important to *not* be told. The money started to come in. Sitting there on her couch, bent, exhausted, Laura Ziskin, for the world to see, was standing tall. Some evenings, David Jacobson, one of the coproducers, would bend down, lift her up, and climb the stairs to lay her down to sleep. She died on June 12, 2011, but not before she made those around her promise to get her last-conceived movie made. They all promised.

With money raised, director, producers, and casting guru Billy Hopkins along with Leah Daniels-Butler began assembling a cast. It's widely acknowledged that actors marvel at the performances Lee Daniels is able to elicit from them. (There's no dissent from the real-life butler's son, Charles Allen, who after seeing Forest Whitaker and Oprah Winfrey play characters inspired by his parents became emotional, later telling me that they had captured the core essence of his mother and father, even if their story had been dramatized for the sake of the film. "They're uncanny," he said of the actors. "They've somehow channeled my mom and dad.") Known for talking at length with his cast about their performances, Daniels also spends countless weeks poring over materials and photographs, immersing himself in the world he will soon commence filming. Actors are told by other actors about his intensity and attention to detail. David Jacobson would make some of the calls to actors' agents as the cast was being assembled. "I would tell agents that by the time this movie is finished, their client would want to pay us for having been in it." He wasn't laughing.

As Laura Ziskin proudly knew, given the film's subject matter, the cast was going to be racially diverse. Oprah Winfrey signed on, then

Forest Whitaker and David Oyelowo. Alan Rickman and Cuba Gooding Jr. and Lenny Kravitz followed. Then came Vanessa Redgrave, Jane
Fonda, and Mariah Carey. The Hollywood trade papers were gushing
over the cast. There were more: Liev Schreiber, James Marsden, John
Cusack, Clarence Williams III, Nelsan Ellis. Many of those who worked
behind the scenes—Ruth Carter in costumes, Andrew Dunn in cine-
matography, Matthew Mungle in makeup—boasted Oscar nominations
and multiple film awards as well. It became common knowledge that
cast and crew took pay cuts to work on the film; otherwise it simply
could not have gotten made. "Many worked for scale," Pam Williams
confided to me. "They just wanted to be in this movie."

One evening on the film set, I asked Danny Strong, a native Cali-
fornian, who had started his career as an actor before turning to screen-
writing, why he was so eager to work on the film. "I'm really passionate
about race in America," he said. "And I thought this film could be a way
to cover African American history from Jim Crow to Obama. I thought
this could be an epic film on race."

There has been much talk over the years in film circles about Hollywood's attempt at civil rights–themed movies. As it is, there have been
just a few. And for the most part, they have been met with scorn. In
1988 came *Mississippi Burning,* which was inspired by the true story
of three murdered civil rights workers in early 1960s Mississippi. The
film made heroes out of the two investigating white FBI agents, which

is where it all went awry. The historical record clearly shows the FBI did not play a heroic role in the Mississippi case, and the movie actually minimized the role of black civil rights workers in the state during the reign of terror there. In 1996 came *Ghosts of Mississippi,* about the probe into the murder of civil rights hero Medgar Evers. Mississippi law enforcement showed little desire to solve the killing. The movie itself focused on the white assistant district attorney—certainly a brave and conscientious man—who reopened the case after it lay unsolved for three decades. Filmmakers, of course, have to make decisions on which particular story to focus on in any multifaceted drama. But a question about *Ghosts* lingered: would not the life story of Medgar Evers have made a compelling drama? Strong was aware of the aftertaste those movies left. "It was easy to avoid that trap," with this movie about a White House butler, he told me. "It wasn't going to be about the noble white man helping the oppressed. This was going to be a story about a black butler and about black kids fighting back in the movement. This was something they did themselves, forcing the presidents to come along with them."

I ARRIVED IN New Orleans a few days before filming on *The Butler* began. After our first chat while I had been in Tennessee, I had first sat down in person with Laura Ziskin and Pam Williams in Washington, DC. Following that, there were also long sessions spent with screenwriter Danny Strong as we visited and talked to real-life butler Eugene Allen. But this was my first visit on the set. It was heartening to sit with the actors, actresses, and other creative people working on *The Butler* and listen to them talk so passionately about why they wanted to work on the film. "They represent the whole black middle class that nobody knew about," Oprah Winfrey said to me one afternoon about the butler and his wife. "It's such a beautiful story."

Everyone associated with the movie was jubilant when Forest Whitaker signed on to play the butler. "My career just wasn't going in the right direction," Whitaker said to me the day before filming got under way. The words sounded a bit jarring coming from the best actor Oscar winner for his galvanizing portrayal of Idi Amin in *The Last King of Scotland*. (Far too many of his movies of late—though Whitaker did not allude to it—have had excruciatingly brief runs in theaters before going to video.) He says how gratified he was when offered the part of the butler: "It's one of the most complicated roles I've ever played." The complexities, he says, stem from the fact that the butler goes from segregation to integration, from president to president, and from decade to decade—in addition to being a father and husband during tumultuous times in American history. "I hope I can meet the challenge" of the role, he said. Whitaker hired a professional butler to teach him the intricacies of the job. (I noticed, on the first day when Whitaker filmed a scene, that he had masterfully adapted Eugene Allen's soft southern accent.)

The role of the butler's son, Louis, is played by the British actor David Oyelowo, who has received acclaim on both sides of the Atlantic but has yet to play that so-called breakout role. Shortly after filming got under way, there was a collective feeling on the set that this might indeed be his chance. He was both magnetic and fierce as the rebellious son of the butler. "It feels divine to be here," he said during lunch one late afternoon during a break in filming. The arc of the film itself—a butler's journey through the White House—had Oyelowo recalling other movies that had claimed the public's attention at one time. "It has elements of *Forrest Gump* and *Gone with the Wind*," he said. "This film pays homage to the foot soldiers." He was well aware of the arduous journey to get the film into production. "It takes the power of people like Lee Daniels and Oprah Winfrey—and this plethora of stars—to get a film like this made," he allowed. Before he landed his part in *The Butler*, Oyelowo was on a roll with appearances in both *The Help* and Spielberg's *Lincoln*, which had not yet been released while he was in New Orleans. "This film is about the butler and his family. There is no white savior."

Much has been made about the actors who wanted to work on the film, but those behind the scenes were just as interested in the project.

The Butler covers time across nine decades and many presidential administrations. (Even though the real-life Eugene Allen worked for eight administrations, the movie only covers five of them.) Such a movie is often referred to as a "period" film and it requires a great deal of historical research. Artists, craftsmen, and designers will work months ahead of filming, coalescing their ideas and suggestions around the director's ultimate vision. The look of the Eisenhower administration is different from the look of the Kennedy administration, and as well with the Nixon and Reagan years. Those different looks have to be conveyed in the furniture, cars, music, and clothing of each era.

Ruth Carter has a highly respected reputation in Hollywood. She earned Oscar nominations for her costume design on Spike Lee's *Malcolm X* and Spielberg's *Amistad.* But she was not taking her acclaim in the industry for granted when she heard about *The Butler.* She was so passionate about getting the job of costume designer that she made her own booklet of clothing designs and shipped it to Lee Daniels. "I fought hard to get the movie," she told me on a short break from her round-the-clock duties on the film set. "The first time I saw a picture of Eugene Allen, I felt like I knew him. I felt like I knew his wife." Carter and dozens of others—cinematographer Andrew Dunn, sound mixer Jay Meagher, graphic artist Kristin Lekki—were all working to shepherd Daniels's vision to the screen.

And what a complex vision. There were days on *The Butler* sets when it felt like you were walking backward through a time machine. There were the COLORED and WHITES ONLY signs in buildings. There were segregated stores and students protesting inside them. There were civil rights marches across bridges and down the middle of streets. There were Klan rallies, and those yelping German shepherd dogs that tore into the clothing of women and children as they protested in the sixties. "People need to capture this before it's gone from everyone's imagination," Tim Galvin, the movie's set designer, was saying about the film's myriad set pieces. Less than two weeks into the production— re-creating the vast tone and texture of the American civil rights movement—he was already feeling it was going to be special. "This movie is so distinctive and meaningful," he acknowledged. "It has such worth to it." There were times, he said, when his crew, along with Daniels, would scout a location. And they'd be told that the bridge they wanted to film on was a bridge where Klansmen had actually attacked blacks. They found a slave cabin that the state of Louisiana had kept restored and used it in the film. "There was another place, the St. James AME Church, where we filmed. Well, it was actually part of the Underground Railroad. Somehow we've been pulled to these places," he said. "There has been a lot of good karma." He goes quiet for a moment. "This is beyond showbiz," he finally uttered.

Still, there were hurdles and endless problems that had to be solved—yesterday, now, first thing tomorrow. *The Butler* faced an enormous one in those early days as the director and production crew first descended upon New Orleans: how to make a movie epic in scope and size on the limited budget they had been able to put together. But Pam Williams and her coproducers knew they had to figure it out. They were all but ready to commence filming, and the movie was too important to turn back now. Williams had even posted a sign in her production office that referenced getting to the finish line: THERE IS NO OTHER OPTION. But finally, while number-crunching the budget again, Williams realized that they simply did not have enough money for the movie Lee Daniels himself had envisioned. The production involved huge set pieces, and Lee, in his meticulousness, had added more production days. That would require more hours of filming, which would require the hiring of more extras. The fear might have brought Williams to her knees. Instead, she took her staff out for shaved ice, a New Orleans delicacy, a summertime treat on a sweltering day. And while out, she thought of the movie, and Laura Ziskin, and the eleven years she had spent at Ziskin's side, and she told herself that this movie had kept Laura alive and fighting. And that she wasn't going to let Laura down. She'd be damned if she was going to pack up the whole crew and return to California. So she swallowed her pride and decided to go back to the investors and ask for more money. "I couldn't deal with her loss," Williams confided to me about Laura Ziskin. She was sitting in a makeup room filled with extras who would be in an upcoming Oval

Office scene. "It was way too wide, too immense. I decided to live in a world of denial and keep pushing to get this movie made as if Laura were still here. Instead of grieving, I put everything into this movie." As did the actors.

Filming bus boycotts, Klan attacks, sit-ins, whites pelting blacks can be viscerally unsettling. Actors appeared emotionally drained after the filming of many such scenes. Even the director wasn't immune. Sometimes it seemed as if every tear that had been dropped from tired eyes by every praying Negro church woman during the civil rights movement in the South was welling anew inside Lee Daniels himself. He'd sometimes sit in silence in his director's chair after an excruciatingly emotional scene. It was as if he had transported himself back to Birmingham or Selma or some Mississippi shack. Then he'd bolt from his chair quick as a cobra because he wanted to tell the actor about something else he wanted in the scene. Later, as he stood in his trademark pajamas, forehead beading with sweat as he watched the scene wind down, a smile would form on his face. He had good reason. He was getting the movie made he had promised Laura Ziskin he'd get made.

It seemed to frighten no one when news came that a hurricane was approaching the city and the production would have to shut down for a spell. The two weeks away provided everyone with needed rest, and when cast and crew returned, filming picked up with the same high energy as before. *The Butler* may have arrived in New Orleans without a distributor, but it would not leave town without one. Harvey Weinstein—who has produced quality film after quality film, many of them Oscar-winning—had been following the trajectory of the movie since it was announced. Word had started to seep out before filming wrapped: Harvey was going to acquire the movie for distribution. "What struck me most about this story," Weinstein told a Hollywood publication, "is the perspective it comes from, which in this case is the butler—a man who was a fly on the wall for decades in the world's most powerful home."

In the end, the story took a nearly five-year journey to the big screen. But it had begun long before, with a black child born on a plantation in Virginia who made his way to the White House: a man who lived long enough to reach his ebony-colored hands inside a voting booth to vote for the man who became the nation's first black president. It involved investors who allowed their conscience to be touched. It found a producer and director who wouldn't give up. *The Butler* became a movement itself.

So here was the movie—made by virtue of a collective and valiant effort—that would lift and carry Laura Ziskin on her way. She flies high above the Hollywood Hills now, her last, final, jubilant wish of a movie dream fulfilled.

Notes

"He stepped out": David Thomson, *The Big Screen* (New York: Farrar, Straus and Giroux, 2012), 22.

"unloosen the energy": Patricia Sullivan, *Lift Every Voice: The NAACP and the Making of the Civil Rights Movement* (New York: The New Press, 2009), 50.

"It is like": Thomson, 24.

"Every Race man": Henry Louis Gates Jr. and Evelyn Brooks Higginbotham, eds., *African American Lives* (New York: Oxford University Press, 2004), 591.

"I did not": James Baldwin, *The Price of the Ticket: Collected Nonfiction 1948–1985* (New York: St. Martin's, 1985), 561.

"It has been": Sidney Poitier, *This Life* (New York: Knopf, 1980), 255.

"We black people": Poitier, 255.

"moving toward two": Mark Harris, *Pictures at a Revolution: Five Movies and the Birth of the New Hollywood* (New York: The Penguin Press, 2008), 403.

FIVE PRESIDENTS
IN THE STRUGGLE

SINCE THE FOUNDING of the nation, few American presidents have escaped the crucible of race. Thomas Jefferson owned slaves; Abraham Lincoln died for the very elimination of slavery. Harry Truman—the first of eight presidents Eugene Allen worked for—came of age in Missouri when lynchings were not at all uncommon there. It was nine children in Little Rock who forced Dwight Eisenhower's administration to unleash federal troops—the first time since Reconstruction—on behalf of black America's plea for equality. Camelot may stylishly swirl in our imaginations, but President John F. Kennedy, tie loosened, was surprisingly introduced to a new kind of movement—civil rights. His successor, Lyndon Johnson, was quick to allow that the bloodshed of the 1960s stretched back to the Civil War, and he met resistance with legislative dynamism. Richard Nixon seemed visibly uncomfortable discussing black issues, though he had a peculiar fondness for the black song-and-dance man Sammy Davis Jr. And who would have imagined Ronald Reagan cornered by a black man imprisoned in South Africa, an ocean away? The five presidents portrayed in *The Butler*—script decisions sometimes have to be ruthless about characters being cut, even if they are presidents—all claimed headlines over the issue of race during their presidencies. During most of those epochal days, the Virginia-born butler of our story was never far from the drama.

IKE

L ITTLE ROCK.
      Those two words would nearly come to define the Eisenhower presidency. The crisis grew, of course, out of the 1954 nation-shaking *Brown v. Board of Education* desegregation ruling. The Supreme Court ruled that America could not continue to discriminate against its black citizens when it came to their educational pursuits. It decreed segregation unlawful. White school districts, however, took their mighty fine time to implement the ruling. Some said they simply would not abide.

Three years later, in the fall of 1957, nine Negro children ascended the steps of Little Rock Central High School in Little Rock, Arkansas. A mob set upon them; the epithets stung like poisoned darts. They were forced to retreat. President Eisenhower was aghast that Arkansas governor Orval Faubus had provided no protection for the children; he had in fact ordered his National Guard to stop them. Ike, military-trained, WWII-tested, dispatched federal troops.

Who knows the depth of scarring the children carried into adulthood? Some have written memoirs, where the pain is evident.

After he had left the White House after his second term, Ike would sometimes stroll the Gettysburg battlefield. He had a companion: his onetime butler Eugene Allen. Eugene had a lot of vacation days, and sometimes he'd go see the president. Ike's servant would serve the both of them. They genuinely seemed to have missed one another.

President Dwight D. Eisenhower

JFK

IT WAS SEPTEMBER 30, 1962, and the hooligans were on their way to Oxford, Mississippi. They swore, by God, that "the nigger," James Meredith, would never integrate the University of Mississippi. Federal courts had ordered the school to comply. When President Kennedy was told that Meredith wouldn't be protected, he grew angry. The state of Mississippi was defying a federal court order. The rioting that erupted was furious. The riotous crowd—both students and outsiders—tossed bricks and bottles at the federal troops Kennedy had sent to the school. Two people, a photographer and a bystander, were killed. But Mississippi would not win this battle. James Meredith successfully integrated Ole Miss, one of the so-called citadels of higher education in the Deep South. Meredith, an Air Force vet who possessed a steely resolve, received sacks of hateful mail and telegrams. There were also kind words. A telegram from the great chanteuse Josephine Baker arrived: GOD IS GOOD JUST AND SURE. WE ARE ALL HAPPY FOR THE RIGHT OF MAN—JOSEPHINE BAKER AND HER CHILDREN WHO REPRESENT THE FIVE CORNERS OF THE WORLD.

"One hundred years of delay have passed since President Lincoln freed the slaves," Kennedy said on national television on June 11, 1963. "Their heirs, their grandsons, are not fully free." The next day, on June 12, 1963, voting rights activist Medgar Evers was murdered in the driveway of his home. Kennedy invited Evers's widow, Myrlie, and the Evers children to the White House for a visit, where Eugene Allen first met them.

Then came the river of tears following that trip to Dallas. In the years to come, a picture would appear in many Negro homes, right

there on the mantel. It was a picture of three who had troubled the waters—Jack Kennedy, Martin Luther King Jr., and Bobby Kennedy—and who were assassinated because of it.

President John F. Kennedy

LBJ

I T WAS A parent's worst nightmare, and worst phone call. Your child
is missing. So began the manhunt. There were three of them, brave
as hell, out to change the world—the world of Mississippi as it was in
that summer of 1964. Andrew Goodman was twenty; James Chaney,
twenty-one; and Michael Schwerner, twenty-four. They had gone to Mississippi with many others to register blacks to vote. But first they had gathered, with about seven hundred others, in Oxford, Ohio, on the campus of
Western College (now merged with across-the-road Miami of Ohio) to be
prepped about conduct in Mississippi: be obedient to authorities, always
let the field office know where you are, avoid the local town after dark.

They were called all kinds of names—"Jewboy," "Communist,"
"nigger"—which is exactly the kind of abuse they were trained for,
along with how to keep their cool. They went missing in Neshoba
County, a particularly hostile area, on June 21. The local authorities
said it was nothing but a hoax, that the "kids" likely just got lazy and
left the area, gone to have fun someplace. President Johnson sent more
than ninety FBI agents into Mississippi.

Many veterans of civil rights in the state knew, from the start, it was unlikely they'd be found alive. A line from *The Butler* script uttered by the butler's wife: "You know those three kids were killed in Mississippi registering black folks."

President Johnson, heroic in the cause of civil rights, got his big Civil Rights Act of 1964 passed that summer. A year later came the Voting Rights Act. None of this completely stopped White House butler Eugene Allen from fretting about his relatives who lived in small southern towns.

There's a lovely monument to the three young martyrs in Oxford, Ohio, the town from which they departed with their dreams that hopeful summer.

President Lyndon B. Johnson

NIXON

I N 1969 PRESIDENT Richard Nixon nominated South Carolina judge Clement Haynsworth to the United States Supreme Court. Of course a lot of digging and scurrying goes on by reporters and busybodies upon announcement of these important nominations. It was discovered that Haynsworth's past judicial decisions favored segregationists. The howls were loud; the nomination was defeated. Nixon—who attended the Duke University School of Law in North Carolina—seemed to have an affinity for southern judges. Undeterred by the Haynsworth debacle, he next nominated Georgia judge G. Harrold Carswell. Again, the digging and probes. Spookily, the Carswell paperwork was just like Haynsworth's: he too had an affinity for ruling in favor of segregationists and bigots. Such nominations would have easily sailed through the Senate in the 1950s. But now the 1960s—and every new black vote throughout the South—had changed a nation, was still changing a nation. Carswell's nomination was defeated as well.

The moniker Tricky Dick gained wider currency in black America after the nominee fiascos. Negro publications had a spirited appetite for such stories, and they had a field day. Did the president not realize that a good many of the butlers and maids at the White House—who were black—had come up from the deeper South during the Great Migration? That the rulings issued by judges like Haynsworth and Carswell could hardly be forgotten?

It is among the first things a domestic hire at the White House

is told: do not talk politics. So they clean and serve with practiced diligence. The first president Eugene and Helene Allen voted for was Franklin D. Roosevelt. They loved voting, that sweetly quiet and powerful form of private expression.

Tea, Mr. President?

President Richard Nixon

REAGAN

WHEN RONALD REAGAN was making movies in Hollywood in the 1940s, a young Nelson Mandela was working in a law firm in Johannesburg, South Africa. At night, in undisclosed locations, he was helping the African National Congress figure ways to bring an end to white rule in the black nation. In time, Mandela took on a larger activist role, which pained the authorities. There were warrants issued for his arrest. Mandela went underground; he became known as the Black Pimpernel, assuming disguises (acting, as it were, for his very *life*) and scooting about the country. His capture in 1962 was worldwide news. He was charged with treason, escaped a hanging, and was eventually sentenced to life in prison.

A decade later, US congressman Ronald Dellums began taking up the Mandela cause, bringing attention to Mandela's plight and the apartheid regime of South Africa, which continued to sell goods to foreign lands while brutalizing and imprisoning its black citizens. Dellums sponsored the Comprehensive Anti-Apartheid Act, which called for Mandela's freedom and an end to South Africa's business practices.

The anti-apartheid movement spread from college campuses to the streets. The years passed, however, and Mandela remained locked away.

In the White House, President Reagan vowed he would not pass the Dellums-sponsored bill. But the movement now was fiery, joined by famous actors and actresses, everyday men and women alike. In 1986, the Comprehensive Anti-Apartheid Act finally passed. It was also Eugene Allen's final year in the White House.

When Nelson Mandela was released from prison in 1990, he embarked on a tour of America to thank his supporters. The nation appeared transfixed. Eugene and Helene watched the televised proceedings. They beamed.

President Ronald Reagan

Acknowledgments

Dawn Davis, editor of this book, contacted me shortly after filming had completed on *The Butler*. She wanted to know if I had any desire to write a book about Eugene Allen. It was the phone call I had been waiting for. I am indebted to her for her clear-eyed determination in bringing this book into existence. Also at Simon & Schuster, I'd like to thank Isolde Sauer, Kyoko Watanabe, Steven Mears, Yona Deshommes, Kimberly Goldstein, Dana Sloan, Jim Thiel, Michael Kwan, and everyone in production who worked so diligently on this book.

My agent, Esther Newberg—our fifth book together—came through in style as I always knew she would.

The director, producers, and actors and actresses abided my presence on the New Orleans set of *The Butler,* for which I will always be grateful. It all really began with a phone call from Laura Ziskin, the legendary producer whose name appears on the dedication page of this chronicle. She forged ahead with a ferocious determination to have a story I wrote adapted, then filmed. She did not live to see the beginning of filming, but her spirit guided everyone. Pam Williams, Laura Ziskin's producing partner and producer of *The Butler*—and whom I shall never forget for her endless kindnesses—proved to me there are saints in Hollywood. Lee Daniels, the director of *The Butler,* has my enduring gratitude for allowing me to watch a genius at work. For taking the time to talk to me about the making of this film, I also thank: Sheila Johnson, Julia Barry, David Oyelowo, Forest Whitaker, Evan Arnold, Oprah Winfrey, Scott Varnado, Ruth Carter, Andrew Dunn, Cuba Gooding Jr., Terrence Howard, Wellington Love, Adam Merims, David Jacobson, Anne Marie Fox, Jay Meagher, Tim Galvin, and Kevin Ladson. And Buddy Patrick, Michael Finley, Bobby Patrick, Earl Stafford, Harry Martin, Charles Bonan, Film Partners, Magnolia-IMC, and Icon Entertainment International, certainly deserve a big round of applause.

Charles Allen, Eugene and Helene Allen's only child, helped in countless and generous ways. Lynn Peterson, Marty Anderson, Steve Reiss, Warren Tyler, Lisa Frazier Page, Mary Jo Green, Michael Coleman, Larry James, Greg Moore, Nina Henderson Moore, Katharine Weymouth, Kevin Merida, Eric Lieberman, Shirley Carswell, Harvey Weinstein and the Weinstein Company, and Tony Stigger also have my gratitude.

About the Authors

A Guggenheim and National Endowment for the Humanities fellow and a former writer for the *Washington Post*, Wil Haygood has written seven nonfiction books. His most recent book, *Showdown: Thurgood Marshall and the Supreme Court Nomination That Changed America*, won multiple literary prizes.

Oscar-nominated director Lee Daniels is perhaps best known for his prizewinning film *Precious: Based on the Novel "Push" by Sapphire*, which received six Academy Award nominations, including best picture, winning in the categories of actress in a supporting role and writing (adapted screenplay). Daniels also produced the Oscar-winning *Monster's Ball* and Fox's highly rated *Empire*, and directed *Shadowboxer* and *The Paperboy*.